The Story
OF REFORM JUDAISM

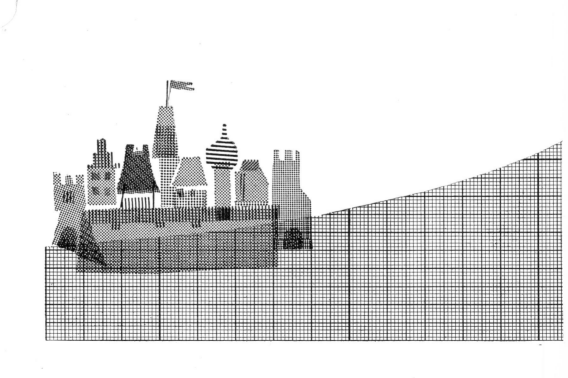

The Story
OF REFORM
JUDAISM

RABBI SYLVAN D. SCHWARTZMAN, Ph.D.

Professor of Jewish Religious Education

Hebrew Union College–Jewish Institute of Religion

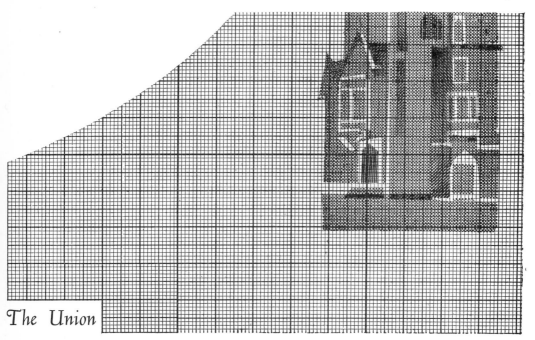

The Union

OF AMERICAN HEBREW CONGREGATIONS, New York

This Book IS PUBLISHED
FROM THE PROCEEDS OF
THE LUDWIG VOGELSTEIN
MEMORIAL FUND

Second Printing, 1955

To Judith and Joel
AND THEIR GENERATION
OF REFORM JEWS

EDITOR'S INTRODUCTION

For many years requests have come from our religious schools for a history of Reform Judaism suited to the needs of boys and girls. *The Story of Reform Judaism* by Rabbi Sylvan D. Schwartzman is the answer to this request. The first book on the subject for the young, it is intended for boys and girls in the eighth grade, and is another example of the pioneering efforts of the Union of American Hebrew Congregations in the field of Jewish education.

Using an interesting technique, Rabbi Schwartzman manages to tell the outstanding events in the rise and development of Reform Judaism in the guise of a series of conversations between two children and among the members of a Reform Jewish family interested in the development of Judaism. Beginning with the discovery of the differences between Orthodoxy and Reform, we are led to a study of the conditions of the Jews in the ghetto and to the gradual changes in Jewish practices which the Reform movement brought about as a result of the adjustment of the Jew to modernism. The author clearly describes the causes of the changes and the results—the founding of the early Reform temples, the changes in the prayer book, and the gradual growth brought about by rabbinical conferences in Europe. The writer then proceeds to the development of Reform Judaism in America. The beginnings of Reform and the early struggles of the movement are vividly depicted. American Reform leaders are introduced and their personalities described. The changes that have taken place in Reform Judaism as a result of the growth of ideas and of the natural processes of development which accompanied the Liberal movement are explained. Finally, the contributions of Reform Judaism to American Jewish life are emphasized.

At the end of each chapter Rabbi Schwartzman has introduced questions for discussion, activities for the youngsters, as well as readings for children and teachers.

This book was first issued in an experimental edition. We are happy to say that it met with favor; hence the present printed edition, which includes a number of suggestions based on classroom experiences of both rabbis and teachers.

May this first *Story of Reform Judaism* for young people increase and intensify their loyalty to the Jewish people and their devotion to Jewish ideals.

EMANUEL GAMORAN

ACKNOWLEDGMENTS

The author wishes to express his personal appreciation to those who have contributed in so many ways to the creation and publication of this first religious school text on the genesis and development of Reform Judaism—

To Drs. Emanuel Gamoran and Jacob R. Marcus for their unstinting helpfulness and wise counsel, and to the other members of the Reading Committee, Dr. Solomon B. Freehof and Rabbi Leon Fram, for their splendid comments and suggestions.

To numbers of rabbis and teachers who have utilized the experimental edition of the book over the past six years and who out of their experience have contributed many worth while suggestions and criticisms which have been incorporated into the revised text.

To the late Dr. David Philipson, revered historian of Reform Judaism, whose monumental work, *The Reform Movement in Judaism*, has long been the major source of the history of the movement and which provided countless insights that proved invaluable in the writing of this volume.

To Ralph Davis whose skill in book designing is evident in the typography and format of this volume. To Mark Heine for the art work in the text.

To Miss Esther Pranikoff, the author's secretary, who painstakingly prepared the final manuscript for publication.

To the following organizations and individuals for the photographs used in the text: American Jewish Archives, pages 101, 103; Beth Elohim Congregation, Charleston, S. C., page 93; Bloch Publishing Co., page 15; Hebrew Union College Museum, pages 17, 23, 33, 40, 47, 58, 87; Jewish Institute of Religion, page 153; Jewish Museum, page 66; Lily Kohler, page 115; National Federation of Temple Sisterhoods, page 144; Union of American Hebrew Congregations, pages 107, 153, 160; Wide World Photos, page 82.

And, finally, to the author's wife, for her innumerable contributions to the preparation of the experimental edition and the final manuscript, and for her constant understanding and encouragement.

The valuable aid of all these and many others is acknowledged with profound and abiding thanks. It is the hope of the author that they will derive satisfaction for their labors from the growing appreciation of Reform Judaism by constantly increasing numbers of our people throughout this land.

S.D.S.

Hebrew Union College–Jewish Institute of Religion
Cincinnati, Ohio

TABLE OF CONTENTS

LIST OF ILLUSTRATIONS

LIST OF CHARTS AND MAPS

The Story
OF REFORM JUDAISM

WHAT'S THE STORY?

Did you know that only 150 years ago there was no such thing as Reform Judaism?

Yet here you are today—a student in a Reform religious school.

You attend temple services with your parents who are members of a Reform congregation.

Your rabbi was graduated from a Reform seminary and belongs to the Central Conference of American Rabbis, an association of more than 600 Reform rabbis.

Your temple's Sisterhood, its Men's Club, and Youth Group are affiliated with strong national Reform organizations.

What's more, this very book you are reading is published by the Union of American Hebrew Congregations, a Reform organization representing over 500 American Reform congregations.

What's that? You have some questions?

— How did Reform Judaism come into being?
— Where did it originate and why?
— What are the religious beliefs of the Reform Jew?
— Who created today's Reform organizations?
— How has American Jewry been influenced by Reform?

There's a fascinating story behind every one of your questions. That's what Betty Friedberg, a Reform Jewish girl of your own age, found out.

And you, too, will discover it as you read

*The Story of
Reform Judaism . . .*

3

1. BETTY ASKS SOME QUESTIONS

Betty Makes a Promise. Saturday morning turned out to be warm and sunny. As Betty Friedberg awoke, she remembered her promise to Mildred. Just yesterday she had agreed to go with her friend to the Sabbath morning services at the Orthodox synagogue. In fact, Mildred was to call for her in less than an hour.

Hurriedly Betty started to get dressed. All the while she couldn't help wondering what an Orthodox synagogue was like. She had never been inside the "shul" as it was generally called. Her parents were Reform Jews and she went with them to temple services. Occasionally, however, her father would attend a Bar Mitzvah or some special service at the Orthodox synagogue. She had meant to ask him about it last night, but had forgotten. It really didn't matter though because soon she would see for herself.

How was it that she had promised to go with Mildred this morning? It came about quite unexpectedly. Yes-

terday afternoon, Betty had told Mildred that she couldn't play tennis because she had to attend a Confirmation rehearsal.

"What's Confirmation?" Mildred surprised her by asking.

"Don't you know about Confirmation?" Betty turned to her friend in amazement. "I thought every Jew knew about the Confirmation ceremony on Shovuos!"

"We're Jews," retorted Mildred, "but we don't have any Confirmation ceremony."

"Well, *we* do," Betty insisted. "We hold Confirmation every year at temple."

"No wonder!" exclaimed Mildred. "You go to the temple! We go to the shul. And at the shul we don't have any Confirmation."

This puzzled Betty. "That's odd," she said, "I thought all Jewish boys and girls were confirmed."

"You're Reform; we're Orthodox. That's the difference."

"All right," Betty agreed, "so I'm

Reform and you're Orthodox. But what does that have to do with Confirmation?"

"Orthodox Jews don't believe in it," was Mildred's reply.

"We're both Jews, aren't we?" Betty demanded. "Why should you believe differently?"

On and on the argument went. Back and forth flew the questions. "What is Orthodox Judaism?" "What is Reform?" "What's the difference between them?" "Which one is right about Confirmation?"

"In our temple," Betty asserted, "we also have a harvest procession at the beginning of Sukos and a Consecration Service for the new boys and girls of the religious school at the close of Sukos. . . ."

Mildred shook her head. "That's not what we do at the shul."

Betty was becoming a little annoyed. "Well, what do you do in your synagogue?"

"Come with me to Shabos services tomorrow morning and you'll see for yourself," retorted Mildred.

"That's a promise," Betty answered.

Off to the Orthodox Synagogue. It was already nine o'clock when Mildred knocked at the door. Betty was all ready to go and soon they were on their way to the synagogue.

The shul was located more than two miles from Betty's house. She suggested to Mildred that they take the bus.

"Oh, no!" was her friend's shocked answer, "we can't ride on Shabos!"

"That's silly," declared Betty, "we always drive to temple on Friday night."

"That's because you're not Orthodox. You're Reform."

Betty didn't say anything but she couldn't help thinking how strange this was. Here they were both Jewish girls and yet each observed her Judaism so differently.

By the time they reached the Orthodox synagogue it was almost ten o'clock. As they climbed the front steps, they could hear the chanting of the cantor. However, instead of entering directly into the synagogue Mildred led Betty up a flight of stairs to the balcony.

Betty Sees a Difference. The girls quickly found seats. Betty looked about and saw only women and girls in the balcony. "Where are the men?" she asked her friend.

Mildred pointed downstairs. Yes, there they were. And all the men were wrapped in *talesim* (prayer-shawls) and wore hats or black skull-caps.

Gradually Betty noticed other things about the shul that were different. To begin with, the Orthodox synagogue had two pulpits! There was the familiar one in front of the Ark, but there was also a larger one right in the center of the synagogue.

The manner of the worship, too, was unfamiliar. As the service proceeded, Betty waited in vain for the music of the organ and the reading of the prayers. Instead, she heard only the voices of the cantor and all-boy choir chanting the prayers, and frequently the congregation would join in singing portions of the service.

The worship was conducted entirely in Hebrew. Betty, of course, had studied Hebrew in the temple religious school and recognized some of the familiar passages, but many of the responses were new to her. Moreover, she had difficulty in following the service because the cantor would recite the prayers too rapidly, and whenever the congregation prayed together some worshippers read faster than others so that the service sounded jumbled.

Betty thumbed through the prayer book which Mildred had handed her. All of the prayers were printed in Hebrew and it was much thicker than her own *Union Prayerbook*.

"You have a much longer service than we have at temple," Betty whispered to her friend.

"Some members have been here since the earlier service at six-thirty this morning," Mildred whispered back. "But the main service didn't begin until nine. It'll probably last until noon."

"Certainly twice as long as ours," Betty thought to herself. She made other comparisons. The Orthodox procedure in reading the Torah was different. After the Scroll of the Law had been taken from the Ark, seven men were called up in turn to the center platform. Each of the men would chant the blessing, and immediately after, the cantor sang a lengthy portion of the Torah section. There was no English translation.

When the Torah had been carried back to the Ark, the rabbi arose and went to the front pulpit to deliver his sermon. He looked very impressive as he stood there wearing his black cap and striped *talis*. Betty was particularly pleased that he spoke in English and she followed his sermon with interest. Later, Mildred told her that occasionally the rabbi would give sermons in Yiddish for the benefit of some of the older members who had come to America as grown-ups and still had difficulty in understanding English.

With the end of the sermon, the cantor resumed his chanting of the service. Here and there Betty made out familiar Hebrew passages and she enjoyed joining with the congregation in the singing of the "Ein Kelohenu" and the final "Adon Olom." Now the service was over and greetings of "Good Shabos" were exchanged. A little later the two girls started for home.

Betty listened intently as her friend spent the walk back explaining some of the Orthodox practices they had just witnessed. All the while Betty couldn't help wondering why Reform Judaism was so different, and when she finally parted from Mildred, she was determined to find out the reason. In fact, she decided to ask Great-Grandfather right away.

Betty Discovers More Differences. As Betty opened the front door of her house, she found Great-Grandfather sitting in the living-room.

"Good Shabos, Great-Grandfather," Betty greeted him.

"Good Shabos, Betty," replied Great-Grandfather. "Your mother told me that you went to the Orthodox synagogue this morning. Did you enjoy the service?"

"Well . . ." Betty faltered, "it . . . it was . . . interesting. But," she hastily added, "it seemed so different." And then she turned to her great-grandfather and asked, "Why should that be? Why do Orthodox Jews observe things so differently?"

Great-Grandfather smiled. "They seem strange to you," said he, "because you're not used to them. You happen to be a Reform Jew."

"I know that, but what does that have to do with it? We're all Jews, aren't we?"

"Of course, Betty," answered Great-Grandfather, "but . . ."

Betty broke in. "Then why, unlike the Orthodox, do we use the organ and have women as well as men sing in our choir? Why don't Orthodox men and women sit together in their synagogue? And why, for instance, don't Reform Jews wear hats and talesim?"

"You're right in pointing out these differences," replied Great-Grandfather. "They're some of the things everyone notices right away. But they really represent something much more fundamental. . . ."

"What do you mean?"

"That Orthodox and Reform Jews have different interpretations of the teachings of Judaism, Betty. Men and women sit together at temple services, for instance, because Reform Judaism insists that Jewish women have the same religious rights as men. That's contrary to Orthodox belief."

"Oh, so that's the reason," exclaimed Betty.

"Yes," asserted Great-Grandfather, "there is much more to your questions than simply differences in synagogue practices. We Reform Jews worship differently because we hold different beliefs about what Judaism teaches."

Some Important Reform Contributions. Great-Grandfather went on. "You know," he told Betty, "because Reform Judaism introduced some of these more modern ideas it has been able to make a number of mighty valuable contributions to American Jewish life. Important new ceremonies, for example. . . ."

"Like Confirmation?" suggested Betty.

"That's right. And the Consecration Service on the last day of Sukos, and many others. Then, too," Great-

Grandfather pointed out, "there's inspiring temple music, much of which has been specially composed for Reform services. And the late Friday evening service—that's strictly a Reform contribution."

"How about the *Union Prayerbook*," added Betty, "and the *Union Hymnal?*"

"You can also include the Union Haggadah," Great-Grandfather said. "All of these are distinct Reform creations. We've taken the lead in building America's most beautiful synagogues; we've pioneered in the field of modern Jewish education. We were among the first to believe that Judaism should be taught to boys and girls in regular classrooms and according to subjects, like history, ceremonies, and current events. The publication of our excellent textbooks for Jewish religious schools is another of Reform's valuable contributions."

"Come to think of it," Betty chimed in, "Reform can take credit for quite a few accomplishments. Just think of all the Reform rabbis who are leaders of important American and world Jewish movements. . . ."

"There are lots of other things, too," Great-Grandfather added. "Our national Reform organizations, for instance, were the first of their kind in American Jewish life—a union of congregations—a permanent rabbinical association—a rabbinical seminary."

"In other words," Betty summed up, "there are really *three* main differences between Orthodox and Reform Judaism—differences in religious practices, differences in the interpretation of Jewish teachings, and the special contributions of Reform to Jewish life."

"Right!" exclaimed Great-Grandfather.

Great-Grandfather Begins a Story. Betty spoke up. "Now I'm even more curious. I'd like to know how all these Reform changes came about."

Great-Grandfather sat quietly for a moment. Then he replied softly, "That's a long story. . . ."

"I still want to know," Betty persisted.

"All right, then. I'll tell you." Great-Grandfather cleared his throat. "This," he started, "is the story of Reform Judaism. . . ."

QUESTIONS FOR DISCUSSION

1. What are some of the practices and beliefs that Reform and Orthodox Judaism share in common?
2. In what ways do Reform and Orthodox Judaism differ?
3. Despite the difficulties in modern times, why do some people prefer to be Orthodox Jews?
4. Why do you prefer being a Reform Jew?
5. In what ways would your life be different if you were an Orthodox Jew?
6. How has the Reform movement benefited the whole of American Jewish life today?

1. Attend a service in an Orthodox synagogue and observe the similarities and differences between it and one in a Reform temple.
2. Invite an Orthodox rabbi or informed layman to discuss and explain various Orthodox practices in which the class is interested.
3. Write an essay on the subject: "Why I choose to be a Reform Jew."

CONOVITZ, MICHAEL, *Dorothy and David Explore Jewish Life,* pp. 175-182.

References for the Teacher

COHON, SAMUEL S., *What We Jews Believe,* pp. 48-50 (Orthodox Judaism), 53-55 (American Judaism).

IDELSOHN, ABRAHAM Z., *The Ceremonies of Judaism,* pp. 79-89 (Orthodox synagogue).

Jewish Encyclopedia, "Reform Judaism from the Point of View of the Reform Jew," Vol. 10, pp. 347-352.

PHILIPSON, DAVID, *The Reform Movement in Judaism,* pp. 1-6 (development of Orthodoxy).

SCHWARTZMAN, SYLVAN D., *Reform Judaism in the Making,* Chap. 1, "Reform and the Jewish Future"; Chap. 17, "This Is Reform Judaism."

Universal Jewish Encyclopedia, "Judaism in America," Vol. 6, pp. 238-243 (Reform and Orthodox Judaism).

2. WHEN GREAT-GREAT-GRANDFATHER WAS A BOY

We Begin Before the Beginning. Betty settled back in the comfortable living-room chair. "Let's see," mused Great-Grandfather, "where shall we begin the story of Reform Judaism?"

"Why, at the beginning, of course," said Betty quickly.

"To tell you the truth, Betty," he replied, "that's not easy to determine. Many people think that Judaism itself has always been a 'reform' movement in the sense that it has constantly adjusted to new ideas and conditions. Others see the beginnings of Reform in such movements as that of the ancient Prophets who tried to 'reform' the Judaism of their times."

"You know," Betty admitted, "I never thought of it that way before. I guess the idea of Reform does go pretty far back in Jewish history." She stopped a moment. "But I was really thinking of the beginning of the Reform movement as we know it today."

"In that case," proposed Great-Grandfather, "we'd better begin *before* the beginning—back in the 1700's when there was no Reform Judaism—just Orthodox Judaism. I recall hearing about those days. When we were little, Father used to tell us about his own childhood in Germany. . . ."

Betty broke in. "You mean *Great-Great*-Grandfather?"

"Yes, Betty. When Great-Great-Grandfather was a boy, our family had dwelt for nearly 500 years in Frankfort-on-the-Main, a large town in southwestern Germany. In fact, there were Jews in Frankfort as early as 1175, but our people had a difficult time of it there. In 1349, for instance, a terrible plague called the Black Death swept Frankfort, and the Jews were accused of having started it. . . ."

"That's silly," Betty exclaimed, "plagues are caused by germs."

"Of course," Great-Grandfather agreed. "Everybody today knows that, but the people in those days

The interior of an old Orthodox synagogue. Note the central pulpit, men praying
with hats and talesim. Compare this with your present day Reform synagogue.

really believed the Jews were responsible. And do you know what they did in revenge? They gathered in mobs, attacked the Jews and destroyed every Jewish home in the city. Afterwards, when the Jews started to rebuild their homes, they were told that they must live in a ghetto, a special section of the town in which all Jews were compelled to dwell."

When Jews Lived in Ghettos. Great-Grandfather went on. "Father used to tell us many stories about the Frankfort ghetto. It consisted of only a single street, fenced off by three gates that could be closed whenever the people wanted the Jews kept inside. There were a number of such times each year—during Easter and on Sundays, for instance—when Jews were forbidden to leave the ghetto.

"Since these Jewish sections were usually surrounded by walls," explained Great-Grandfather, "the ghettos could not expand. As time passed the number of Jews would increase but the area of the ghetto remained the same. In Frankfort, the Jews tried to provide more room by filling in an old moat that lay within their quarter and adding extra stories to their houses. But this was by no means sufficient to meet their needs. Eventually the government intervened to end the problem. It allowed only six new families a year to move into the ghetto and, that too many children might not be born, it limited the number of Jewish mar-

riages during any year to twelve."

"How awful!" cried Betty.

"Worst of all," Great-Grandfather pointed out, "life in the ghetto was dangerous. Jews never knew when they might be attacked by an angry mob. If the ghetto were walled, it frequently served as a protection against enemies outside. But sometimes the very walls became a trap, for once the crowd had broken down the gates and come pouring in, the Jews had no way of escape.

"That almost happened to our family in 1614," Great-Grandfather related. "In that year a scoundrel named Fettmilch stirred up his followers against the Jews. This Fettmilch had become the leader of a religious group whom the rulers of Frankfort disliked, and in order to show how strong he and his supporters were, he challenged the power of the city authorities by organizing riots against the Jews. The town officials were unable to stop him when he and his followers broke into the ghetto and set fire to the synagogue. They ripped up the Torahs, smashed Jewish gravestones, and sought to kill every Jew. While a number of Christians bravely protected the Jews and even sheltered some in their homes, most of Frankfort Jewry had to flee for their lives. Fortunately our family escaped.

"But even when our people were not under attack," Great-Grandfather continued, "they were at a disadvantage in other ways. For outside the ghetto walls a feudal system, closely linked with the Christian religion, regulated the lives of the people. According to this feudal system farmers could receive the right to their land only by swearing a Christian oath of loyalty to their noble or king. Thus, Jews could not become farmers. And, in order to qualify as a worker in a craft or shop, one had to become a member of a guild which, however, admitted only Christians. Social and political life, too, were centered about the Church. Even the courts required a witness to testify upon an oath as a Christian."

Who Protected the Jews? "Didn't the Jews have any rights at all?" Betty asked.

"Interestingly enough, the European kings usually granted them the right of protection," Great-Grandfather answered, "since they considered Jews a most valuable financial asset. Each year our people were forced to pay much heavier taxes than Christians, and in spite of the general poverty, Jews were often compelled to 'loan' the kings large sums of money which were almost never paid back.

"Jews, you see, were not citizens either of the countries in which they lived or of the lands in which they were born. In fact, our people hadn't enjoyed citizenship in any European country since the time of the Roman Empire, about the fourth century, and for nearly fourteen hundred years they were at the mercy of the rulers who considered them their special 'property.' As long as his Jews were a source of ready cash, it was to the king's advantage to protect them. But sometimes a sudden uprising against the ghetto caught the royal guards unprepared and the mob succeeded in breaking in. Or, should the Jews be unable to provide the king with the money he demanded, he might order them out of the country. The kings of France actually expelled their Jews three times in less than ninety years."

Betty fumed. "Our people should have rebelled against those kings!"

"Against their armies?" Great-Grandfather asked pointedly. "Or against the ready mobs they could incite against the ghettos? Oh, no, Betty, Jews were willing to pay the heaviest taxes if the kings would only allow them to live in peace. They knew how terrible an expulsion was —no place to go, no country willing to accept them, many dying of hunger and disease in the long search for a new home. At best, those who managed to receive refuge elsewhere found conditions there no different."

Why Jews Were Disliked. Betty was puzzled. "I don't understand why our people were so disliked," she said to Great-Grandfather.

"There were several reasons," he answered, "but none was really the fault of the Jews. For one thing, they were persecuted because they refused to become Christians. Practically all Europeans were Christians, and Jews were looked upon as stubborn and even wicked for remaining loyal to Judaism. Some Christian leaders felt it their duty to protect their people against 'Judaizing' as they called it, by forbidding all Christians to have any contacts with the Jew or his faith. They deliberately passed cruel laws designed to make the Jews the outcasts of European society by compelling them to wear special hats or yellow badges on their clothes that everyone might immediately identify them as the 'despised' Jews. Jews were prohibited from entering many businesses and professions; they weren't permitted to own land, and they had to live in ghettos. Some of the Christian leaders hoped that persecution would induce many Jews to give up their religion, especially since they were offered complete freedom if they would accept Christianity. To begin with, therefore, it was their loyalty to Judaism which caused our people to be disliked.

"Then, too, because Jews were isolated in ghettos people spread all kinds of fantastic tales about them. Jews were said to use Christian blood in their celebration of Passover, and there was the popular legend that Jews would steal into churches and secretly stab the holy wafers symbolizing the body of Jesus which, of course, was considered a terrible crime against Christianity. People were ready to believe almost any-

An old print showing medieval Jews sworn in court. Note the special hats worn by these early Jews to distinguish them from the rest of the population.

thing about the relatively unknown and hence 'mysterious' Jews.

"The fact that some Jews were money-lenders became another reason for the unpopularity of our people. Because Jews were barred from most of the normal occupations, a few turned to money-lending for a living since that was one of the few businesses prohibited by church law to Christians but not forbidden to Jews. Money-lenders are never popular, particularly with the people who borrow from them, and because they were Jewish they were doubly disliked. As a consequence hatred was heaped upon all Jews.

"Finally," Great-Grandfather went on, "because they were so universally unpopular Jews served as a convenient scapegoat. If bad economic conditions became acute, kings who were afraid of uprisings by the people would blame the trouble on the Jews. Ambitious men who sought power would attract popular attention by leading attacks against the Jews. Since they were in no position to defend themselves, Jews offered an easy target for their enemies."

"It's amazing that our people could go on living under these terrible conditions," Betty observed.

"It would have been utterly impossible," agreed Great-Grandfather, "had it not been for their Jewish way of life which made survival possible."

How Jewish Life Promoted Survival. "Yes," Great-Grandfather repeated, "it was the creation of an effective Jewish community life that made existence bearable. Confined to the ghetto, Jews developed a wonderfully organized community of their own. They provided themselves with schools in which boys concentrated upon Jewish learning rather than general subjects such as geography, languages, or mathematics. The school was conducted in the synagogue, and the main textbooks were the Bible, the Talmud, and other great Jewish works.

"The ghetto contained other institutions as well. In practically every ghetto Jews organized themselves for self-government, for the collection of charity and taxes, and for the distribution of relief. In Frankfort, for instance, the Jewish community had its own cemetery, bakery, social hall, hospital, and bath house. Frankfort Jewry also elected twelve elders who conducted the affairs of the community. They established courts presided over by the rabbis or their appointees who enforced community regulations as well as the laws of the Talmud, Shulchan Aruch, and other code books. Through the rabbinical use of the 'cherem' or excommunication, any Jew found guilty of violating the law or endangering the safety of fellow Jews could be expelled from the community. You can imagine the seriousness of this punishment! The guilty party would be cut off from all contact with fellow Jews; he would have to live by himself in the hostile community outside.

"Within the ghetto, Jews also developed a language of their own— Judeo-German, a mixture of German and Hebrew. It was natural that they should feel all the more at home among their fellow Jews now that there was difficulty in speaking the language of the outside community.

"However, above all else, it was their religion which enabled our people to endure their ghetto existence. My father often spoke of the wonderful religious spirit of the

The Frankfort Ghetto. Ghettos like this were actually cities within cities where Jews lived and worked.

ghetto—how all Jews would come to the synagogue for the three services every day, how every merchant closed his shop during Shabos, and each Jew observed all of the Jewish holidays. And how the Jewish festivals were celebrated—the joy that reigned on Passover, Sukos, Shovuos, Chanuko and Purim—the solemnity that marked the ghetto on the High Holydays and on various fast days like the Ninth of Ov! Because the Jews lived solely within their own community, it was so much easier for everyone to observe all of the Jewish customs.

"Jewish community life, too, was a source of special pride that helped our people bear their humiliations.

When Jews compared their life in the ghetto with that outside, they discovered the many advantages that they enjoyed. Jews were generally far better educated, for while many of the Christians were illiterate, practically every Jew could read and write. Outside the ghetto robbery and murder were common, but very few Jews committed serious crimes. Desertion and ill-treatment of wives and children were frequent among Europeans, but to the Jew family life was regarded as sacred. All of this gave the Jews a feeling of being indeed a 'Chosen People,' a people especially blessed by God, and a people destined some day to receive even greater rewards!"

The Promise of Greater Rewards. "Yes," Great-Grandfather repeated, "Jews firmly believed that the future would surely bring them wonderful rewards. They were convinced that the present suffering would soon end and God would restore them to Palestine. There, in their ancient homeland, they would rebuild the Temple, reintroduce the ancient sacrifices and reestablish their own Jewish kingdom under the Messiah, a descendant of King David. Then, at last, Israel would enjoy peace, freedom, and prosperity forever. Even the Jewish dead would return to life and join their people in Palestine."

"When was this to happen?" asked Betty.

"That, the people said, was for God to determine. Meanwhile our people continued to pray for Elijah to appear and announce the coming of the Messiah. This custom has continued down to the present, for even today all Jews greet Elijah at the Passover Seder with the hope that his presence will usher in the Messianic Age.

"But our people believed in still another reward," Great-Grandfather told Betty. "After death, the soul of each Jew, who during his lifetime had been just and peace-loving and had faithfully observed every Jewish law and practice, would be certain to ascend to the heavenly 'Garden of Eden' where God Himself dwelt. . . ."

What! No Changes Allowed? Betty interrupted. "Do you mean that *every* law had to be observed?" she asked.

"Yes, indeed," he asserted. "Every commandment was important. All of them had to be obeyed."

"Such as not riding on the Sabbath?" questioned Betty.

"Surely. But that wasn't so difficult in the ghetto where everyone lived near the synagogue."

"And in the synagogue," Betty went on with her questions, "men and women had to sit apart?"

Great-Grandfather nodded.

"And they must pray only in Hebrew and not use the organ?"

"That's right," said Great-Grandfather.

"Why," Betty exclaimed, "these are the very things the Orthodox still do! Do you mean that their practice of Judaism hasn't changed at all since Great-Great-Grandfather was a boy?"

"No, Betty. Officially, nothing has been changed."

"But," Betty protested, "why shouldn't Judaism change? Jewish life today is certainly different from what it used to be. We don't live in ghettos any more. Why can't our religion keep up with the times? Why can't we introduce new ceremonies and modernize some of the old beliefs and practices?"

Great-Grandfather smiled sympathetically. "You know, Betty, those are some of the very questions that many Jews began to ask when our people were freed from the ghettos. It's because those Jews asked them that you're a Reform Jew today. . . ."

"So that's the way Reform Judaism began!" cried Betty. "Because people asked questions—just like me!"

"Yes," Great-Grandfather chuckled, "they dared to ask questions, just like you." His face grew serious. "But, Betty, sometimes questions can be very shocking."

"Shocking? Not really!"

Great-Grandfather leaned forward. "In those days such questions were not only shocking . . . they were actually considered dangerous, as you will shortly see. . . ."

QUESTIONS FOR DISCUSSION

1. Why is it difficult to determine when Reform Judaism really began?
2. Compared to present-day American Jewish life, what advantages and disadvantages did the medieval Jew possess?
3. Why was it impossible for Reform Judaism to develop in ghetto days?
4. What elements found in medieval Jewish life are still present today?
5. How do the reasons given for the dislike of the medieval Jew compare with those raised by modern anti-Semites?
6. In what ways does the Reform Judaism of today differ from the Judaism of the ghetto?

SUGGESTED ACTIVITIES

1. Conduct a debate on the subject: "*Resolved,* That Jewish life was more wholesome in ghetto times than today."
2. Invite an elderly person who spent his youth in Eastern Europe to describe his Jewish life there.
3. Prepare a series of exhibits which contrast the life of the medieval and modern Jew.

ADDITIONAL READINGS FOR PUPILS

FEUER, LEON I. and AZRIEL EISENBERG, *Jewish Literature Since the Bible, II,* pp. 107-120, 125-128, 131-132, 143-146.

GITTELSOHN, ROLAND B., *Modern Jewish Problems,* pp. 196-197 (A).

GOLUB, JACOB S. and ALAN S. GREEN, *A Short History of the Jews, II,* pp. 41-53.

MARCUS, JACOB R., *The Jew in the Medieval World,* pp. 24-32, 34-40, 43-47, 75-79, 86-87, 89-91, 121-130, 137-141, 155-158, 200-204, 212-221, 378-380.

SOLOFF, MORDECAI I., *How the Jewish People Lives Today,* pp. 41-47, 56-76, 130.

References for the Teacher

ABRAHAMS, ISRAEL, *Jewish Life in the Middle Ages,* Chap. 2, "Life in the Synagogue"; Chap. 3, "Communal Organization"; Chap. 4, "Institution of the Ghetto"; Chap. 5, "Social Morality"; Chap. 16, "The Jewish Badge"; Chaps. 17 and 18, "Private and Communal Charities."

FREIMANN, A., and F. KRACAUER, *History of the Jews in Frankfort,* Chap. 6, "The Fettmilch Insurrection."

Jewish Encyclopedia, "Frankfort-on-the-Main," Vol. 5, pp. 484-489; "Ghetto," Vol. 5, pp. 652-655.

ROTH, CECIL, *A Bird's-Eye View of Jewish History,* Chap. 25, "Life in the Ghetto."

SACHAR, ABRAM L., *A History of the Jews,* Chap. 19, "The Jew in the Medieval World."

SCHWARTZMAN, SYLVAN D., *Reform Judaism in the Making,* Chap. 2, "The Jew of Medieval Europe."

Universal Jewish Encyclopedia, "Frankfort on Main," Vol. 4, pp. 400-402; "Ghetto," Vol. 4, pp. 597-603.

3. GREAT-GREAT-GRANDFATHER IS SHOCKED!

Why Orthodox Judaism Couldn't Change. "I can't see what's so shocking or dangerous about asking questions," Betty confided to her great-grandfather. "No one is shocked at me, and I'm always asking all sorts of questions."

Great-Grandfather laughed. "Oh, that's different," he said. "But over many centuries Judaism had developed set religious practices and when, after such a long time, some Jews commenced to raise questions about these, it semed very startling. Post-Biblical Judaism, you see, established the fundamental Jewish laws with the completion of the Talmud, about the year 500 of the Common Era. While it is true that from time to time afterwards interpretations by various rabbis modified some of these regulations, most Jews considered their religious practices as something very old and permanent. Therefore, they looked upon questions which sought to make real changes in Jewish practice as 'sinful.' "

"But why should they call that 'sinful'?" Betty wanted to know.

"Because in those days Jews believed that the whole of Jewish law had been established by God for all times," he replied. "To them every religious ceremony and belief was the 'word of God.' The Bible was called the 'Written Law'; the rabbis' decisions in the Talmud and other rabbinical writings were known as the 'Oral Law.' Both the Oral Law and Written Law were believed to have been handed down by God, and as such, could be changed only by God. Man had no right to alter them in their fundamentals. You can begin to understand, then, why people became so upset over any suggestion that Judaism be greatly modified to meet the needs of modern life. . . ."

Great-Grandfather rose from his chair. "Wait here a moment," he said as he turned to leave the living-room. "I'll let you see for yourself what your great-great-grandfather had to say on the subject."

21

Great-Grandfather Reads from a Diary. Betty waited impatiently for great-great-grandfather's diary. He hadn't been gone long when he came back carrying an old leather-covered volume. Its binding was very worn and some of the pages were badly frayed. As he unfastened the heavy covers, Betty could see the yellowed leaves.

She couldn't restrain her curiosity. "What's that, Great-Grandfather?"

"This," he answered, "is your great-great-grandfather's diary. He kept a personal record of everything that went on." Great-Grandfather thumbed through several pages. Then he found what he was looking for and started to read. . . .

"This is dated in the year 1782:

" 'Father came home tonight very disturbed. All of us, too, were disquieted at the news he brought. Today, it seems, our rabbi of Frankfort, Rabbi Phineas Levi Horowitz, called a meeting of the Jewish elders and demanded that they forbid our people to read Moses Mendelssohn's new German translation of the Bible. Any Jew reading the Bible in a language other than Hebrew, our rabbi said, is guilty of a terrible sin.

" 'Father told the meeting that it was hard for him to believe that Moses Mendelssohn would cause any Jew to sin, for Mendelssohn has always been regarded as one of our greatest men, a distinguished thinker and a devoted Jew.

" 'Father defended Mendelssohn with the facts that he knew about him. Born in 1729 in Dessau, Germany, Mendelssohn carried on his studies in Berlin. There he learned not only the tradi-

tional Jewish writings but also mathematics, logic and German literature. Because he was gifted with such a fine mind and quickly learned to speak German fluently, he became associated with many outstanding writers and scholars, and Lessing, the famous German dramatist, is a particularly close friend of his. Mendelssohn became especially well known after winning the important Berlin Academy Prize for his essay—something unheard of for a Jew!

" 'But he has always shown himself to be a pious and staunch Jew, Father insisted. Once, after becoming famous, an overly-zealous Christian, John Lavater, tried to convert him to Christianity. Mendelssohn absolutely refused to hear of it.

" 'At this point one of the group interrupted Father. Wasn't Mendelssohn openly criticizing certain weaknesses in Judaism?

" 'Yes, Father answered, it was true that Mendelssohn said that he had noticed certain human additions and abuses in his religion, but these could surely be corrected without any danger to Judaism. In fact, he felt it his duty to remedy them. If, for instance, he could improve the German education of his fellow Jews, he was sure that the outside world would more readily accept them. His own experience seemed to prove his argument.

" 'The first step, he felt, was to translate the Bible into German so that Jews who knew the Bible in Hebrew would easily learn to read it in the new language. Soon they would understand and speak German and become better acquainted with their German neighbors. Surely, Mendelssohn reasoned, the German people would come to appreciate the Jews and accept them as citizens. In what way, Father asked the group, was this a sin against Judaism?

" 'Angrily, Rabbi Horowitz rose to

Moses Mendelssohn

his feet. He informed the Frankfort elders that it was against this very translation of the Bible that he most strongly objected. He wanted the group to know that this was Mendelssohn's way of trying to undermine their faith. Hadn't he already criticized Judaism? Wasn't he saying that their religion had human abuses which he intended to correct? Furthermore, hadn't he agreed with the Duke of Mecklenburg-Schwerin that all burials should be delayed a day or two lest someone believed dead be accidently buried alive? Thus Mendelssohn was guilty of violating Jewish law which demanded burial as soon as possible.

" 'Rabbi Horowitz bitterly condemned Mendelssohn's translation of the Bible. Why, if Jewish boys were allowed to study it, they would be learning the German language instead of the contents of the Bible! Eventually, too, they might no longer be familiar with Hebrew.

" 'Most of the elders of Frankfort agreed with the rabbi, and many in the community seem greatly disturbed by the action of Moses Mendelssohn.' "

Great-Grandfather turned several pages. "Listen to this, Betty." It was written a few months later:

" 'The ghetto is buzzing with exciting news. Not since Lessing wrote his play, *Nathan the Wise*, and made Moses Mendelssohn its hero have we received such glad tidings. For Emperor Joseph II of Austria has just decreed that Jews are now permitted to open factories and engage in every kind of trade. Jews need no longer wear any special garment or badge and may henceforth send their children to the public schools.

" 'This news, too, comes only a short while after the Prussian Councilor of State, Christian Wilhelm von Dohm, published his book asking that Jews be given equal rights and freedom of religion and occupation.

" 'With two such happenings within a single year no wonder Frankfort Jewry is rejoicing. Perhaps Germany, too, will begin adopting some of the more enlightened Austrian laws. . .'

"This entry is dated 1783," Great-Grandfather told Betty after he had skipped a number of pages in the diary:

" 'Moses Mendelssohn has finally completed his German translation of the Bible.

" 'Most of the important rabbis of Europe are threatening to punish anyone found reading his translation, but more and more Jews are secretly studying it. Just this morning I saw one of our Jewish students reading a copy behind a large volume of the Talmud. Gradually, too, one hears Jews speaking German and quoting lines of German poetry.

" 'It may be that Mendelssohn has the right idea after all. Perhaps if the

German people see that we Jews are learning the language and show a greater interest in our country, they may change some of their unfavorable laws and even come to accept us as citizens. . . .' "

Judaism Must Adjust. "Then Mendelssohn was correct after all!" exclaimed Betty. "And that Frankfort rabbi was wrong."

Great-Grandfather put down the diary. "Of course Mendelssohn was right, Betty, in trying to help his people, but Rabbi Horowitz wasn't entirely wrong either. The rabbi of Frankfort was afraid that once the Jews of the ghetto became accustomed to the outside world some of their Jewish practices would undergo changes. German-speaking Jews, for example, would no longer be satisfied with an all-Hebrew service, and would demand some prayers in German."

"That's natural," Betty admitted. "Since they would be living differently, they would begin worshipping differently." She paused and then said, "But you told me this was going to be a shocking story. What's so shocking about all this?"

"You'll see," promised Great-Grandfather. "Listen to this portion of Great-Great-Grandfather's diary. It was written in 1817:

" 'I have just returned home from a business trip to Berlin. What an exciting city, but what a shocking one as far as Judaism is concerned!

" 'So many of our wealthy, cultured Jewish families are forsaking the faith of their fathers. Now it is Henrietta Herz, wife of a fine Jewish physician, who has become converted to Christianity.

" 'And poor dead Moses Mendelssohn! How ashamed he would have been had he known that his own daughters, Dorothea and Henrietta, would become Catholics. Rachel Levin, too, has left the faith to marry a Prussian diplomat.

" 'Among some prominent Berlin Jews it is considered fashionable to snub fellow Jews and to have homes that no longer reflect the spirit of Jewish observance.

" 'What will become of our people and our religion? Our young people are beginning to neglect their Jewish education in favor of German culture. Must Judaism be destroyed by the new freedom? We hope not!

" 'Perhaps this is only the immediate reaction to our new-found liberty. Meanwhile, however, we cannot help being outraged by the scandals of Berlin and other large Jewish centers.

" 'Some of the rabbis who cautioned against Mendelssohn's German translation of the Bible see today's happenings as proof of their warnings and are seeking to prevent all Jews from studying modern culture. In fact, a number even objected to the acceptance of freedom offered the Jews of Amsterdam in 1795!' "

"Do you mean," exclaimed Betty, "that they preferred having Jews live in ghettos? Couldn't our people enjoy freedom and still be faithful to Judaism?" she asked in amazement.

Great-Grandfather smiled. "Aren't you a loyal Jew and a good American?"

Betty stopped short. Then she

broke into a grin. "I forgot all about that," she laughed.

"Still you must understand, Betty, that the example of Berlin was frightening to the rabbis. They didn't realize that it was possible for Jews to have both freedom and Judaism."

Betty took a guess. "Was that where Reform Judaism came on the scene?" she asked.

"No, not yet," Great-Grandfather restrained her. "We don't come to Reform Judaism yet. First we've got a revolution to fight. . . ."

Coming: A Revolution! "Well," said Betty, highly pleased at Great-Grandfather's last remark, "I'm certainly glad to hear we finally rose up against those heartless kings. . . ."

"Hold on there a minute!" shouted Great-Grandfather. "We Jews didn't revolt. It was the French."

Betty showed her disappointment. "Oh," she said, "I thought it was like the Maccabees—a *Jewish* rebellion."

"No, this happens to be the French Revolution," replied Great-Grandfather, "but it turned out to be a Jewish revolution after all."

This baffled Betty. "You're very confusing," she complained. "A Jewish . . . and not a Jewish . . . revolution. I don't understand."

"You will," he reassured her with a pat, "after lunch. It would be far too much excitement on an empty stomach," he teased.

"Well, come on," Betty called as she grabbed hold of Great-Grand-father's arm and tried to pull him up from the chair. "Let's hurry up and eat. I want to hear more about this revolution. . . ."

QUESTIONS FOR DISCUSSION

1. What developments in late eighteenth century Europe prompted some Jews to seek changes in Judaism?

2. What were the principal objections to changes in Judaism?

3. Why, despite strong Jewish opposition, did Moses Mendelssohn insist upon translating the Bible into German?

4. How did Moses Mendelssohn pave the way for the development of Reform Judaism?

5. In what ways is the influence of Moses Mendelssohn seen in American Jewish life today?

6. How did the developments which took place during and after Mendelssohn's lifetime affect Jewish life?

SUGGESTED ACTIVITIES

1. Conduct a trial of Moses Mendelssohn for translating the Bible into German and prepare statements for the prosecution and defense.

2. Present a news broadcast dealing with the completion of Moses Mendelssohn's translation of the Bible.

3. Prepare a script dramatizing important scenes from the life of Moses Mendelssohn.

ADDITIONAL READINGS FOR PUPILS

FEUER, LEON I. and AZRIEL EISENBERG, *Jewish Literature Since the Bible, II*, pp. 157-160, 164-170.

GOLUB, JACOB S. and ALAN S. GREEN, *A Short History of the Jews, III*, pp. 1-9, 14-18.

LURIE, ROSE G., *The Great March, II*, pp. 77-88.

SOLOFF, MORDECAI I., *How the Jewish People Lives Today*, pp. 108-123.

References for the Teacher

GRAETZ, HEINRICH, *History of the Jews*, "The Measfim and the Judaeo-Christian Salon," Vol. 5, Chap. 10.

Jewish Encyclopedia, "Gotthold Ephraim Lessing," Vol. 8, p. 14; "Moses Mendelssohn," Vol. 8, pp. 479-485.

PHILIPSON, DAVID, *The Reform Movement in Judaism*, pp. 6-11 (Mendelssohn and Friedlander).

SACHAR, ABRAM L., *A History of the Jews*, pp. 266-272 (Moses Mendelssohn).

SCHWARTZMAN, SYLVAN D., *Reform Judaism in the Making*, Chap. 3, "The First Rays of Freedom."

Universal Jewish Encyclopedia, "Dorothea Mendelssohn," Vol. 7, p. 470; "Henriette Mendelssohn," Vol. 7, p. 471; "Moses Mendelssohn," Vol. 7, pp. 471-474; "Rahel Varnhagen von Ense" (Rachel Levin), Vol. 10, p. 396.

4. FORWARD MARCH!

Betty Gets Some Ammunition. When lunch was over, Betty tugged impatiently at Great-Grandfather. "Let's hurry up," she urged. "We've got a revolution on our hands . . . remember?"

"Meet me in the living-room," Great-Grandfather told her. "I'll be there presently with plenty of ammunition."

"Ammunition?" Betty asked herself, "what on earth can he mean?"

In a few minutes, Great-Grandfather made his appearance, and he handed Betty two books. "Here's your ammunition," he said.

The girl showed her disappointment. "But . . . but these are only books," she protested.

"Right you are. Books—good Jewish weapons," answered Great-Grandfather. "And that's a fine way to go through the French Revolution this Shabos . . . reading." And with that he left the room.

Betty opened the first book that

Great-Grandfather had given her. It was a history of modern Europe and she saw that it commenced with a chapter on the French Revolution. "So modern times begin with the French Revolution," she thought aloud. "That explains why Reform Judaism comes later." Then, sprawling herself comfortably in the chair, Betty started to read.

Why the French People Revolted. The opening pages gave some of the reasons for the outbreak of the Revolution in 1789. The main cause seemed to be the French people's growing hatred of the "feudal" system. Under the feudal system, France, like all of the other countries of Europe, was tightly controlled by the king and his nobles. Practically all French land was owned by the nobility and the Church. The farmers were required to swear oaths of obedience to the particular noble whose land they occupied. The nobility, in turn, swore to be faithful to their overlord, the king.

In the cities, workingmen, the bosses as well as the hired workers, were enrolled in guilds, special societies organized by trades. These guilds carried on practically all manufacturing and were also part of the feudal system. Their members, too, had to promise obedience to the king. Feudal oaths to the king and his nobility were fulfilled by paying heavy taxes, serving in the armies of the nobility, working on the highways, and respecting the royal laws. In fact, strict obedience to every command of the king and his nobles was required.

In those days there was no such thing as the popular election of rulers. Kings actually believed that God alone had appointed them to reign and their kingship was to be handed down for all times from father to son. Hence, they felt no responsibility to the people for any of their acts. Furthermore, because the people had sworn to obey them, they did not hesitate to imprison without trial anyone who objected to their conduct.

As European trade became more wide-spread, a large class of well-to-do Frenchmen began to appear—lawyers, shopkeepers, traders, scientists, ship-owners, inventors. The "middle class," as this group was called, enjoyed considerable wealth but had very little authority since the king and his nobles possessed complete political power. There was no place for the middle class within the feudal system; nor did its members enjoy any influence at the royal court. Naturally, therefore, this growing middle class desired a change of government and sought a new political system which would give it proper representation in the running of the country.

There was another group of Frenchmen, too, that seethed with discontent—the hard-working peasants, called "serfs" in the feudal system. They complained bitterly against the payment of heavy taxes to the king and his nobles; they objected to the wasteful wars in which they were compelled to risk their lives; and they were especially outraged by the royal luxuries which squandered their hard-earned tax money. Thus the farmers of France were ready to listen to anyone who promised them better government.

How France Won Its Freedom. By the year 1788, the French king, Louis xvi, was desperate. He and his predecessors had squandered so much money that the government was threatened with bankruptcy unless it could quickly obtain new and heavier taxes from the French people. But the people flatly refused. Bad harvests, a severe winter, and high prices had already embittered them, and they announced that they would grant the king no new taxes unless they or their representatives were officially invited to discuss the matter.

Louis xvi had little choice. If he wanted additional funds he would have to call an assembly of the peoples' representatives—the Estates-General, as it was named. At the same time he began receiving long lists of the people's grievances. Frenchmen were protesting against imprisonment without trial; they condemned the many feudal taxes which were exacted from them. Furthermore, they demanded a bill of rights that would guarantee them freedom of worship, assembly, and speech.

The Estates-General was ordered to meet, and the delegates, one of whom was Lafayette, a hero of the American Revolution, gathered on May 5, 1789. They promptly declared themselves a National Assembly representing the people of France. Fearing that this was a threat to his power, the king surrounded the assembly place with his soldiers, and the delegates assumed that the king intended to put an end to their meeting. In protest the people of Paris rioted and, on July 14, stormed the Bastille, a fortress in which some innocent Frenchmen were imprisoned. The king was powerless to stop them. The French Revolution was on!

All over France the people removed the king's officials from office. Then, shouting the popular slogan of the Revolution, "Liberty, Fraternity, Equality!" hostile mobs attacked the nobles, killing some, forcing others to flee the country. Even the king and queen were taken prisoner.

The National Assembly promptly proclaimed an end to the feudal system. No longer were there to be nobles, guilds, or serfs in France. Influenced by the example of the American Revolution and its Declaration of Independence of 1776, the French National Assembly produced a "Declaration of the Rights of Man" which began, "Men are born and remain free and equal in rights." It went on to guarantee all Frenchmen complete freedom of religion, press, assembly, and speech, and to provide for a representative form of government for France.

Europe's Kings Fight Back. It was natural that other European kings and nobles should be alarmed by what was taking place in France. They felt their own position threatened as long as the revolt against French royalty was succeeding. Thus, when the plot of the French king and queen to escape from France failed, the kings of Austria and Prussia announced their determination to restore King Louis xvi to his throne even against the will of the French people.

This defiance led the National Assembly to declare war on Austria, and, in a bold challenge to the might of the European monarchs, the French government put the king and queen on trial and had them executed. In an official proclamation, it announced to the oppressed people of Europe that France would help all countries that wanted freedom from tyrants.

The execution of the French king and queen and the threat to royalty everywhere contained in the Assembly's proclamation soon brought Great Britain, Spain, Holland, Sardinia, and Prussia into the war against France.

Enter: Napoleon Bonaparte. It was then that the son of a poor Corsican lawyer, Napoleon Bonaparte, a little-known officer in the French army, began his rise to power. Appointed to command the French army of Italy, he won brilliant victories over both Austria and Sardinia and forced them to sue for peace. In 1799, when Austria, Russia, and Great Britain declared war on France for the second time, Napoleon was placed at the head of the entire French army. He was now the most powerful figure in France and the outstanding victories of this war, as well as of others that followed, made him a popular hero. At the end of 1804, Napoleon was crowned Emperor of France.

Wherever Napoleon's armies marched, they shouted the revolutionary slogan, "Liberty, Fraternity, Equality!" and introduced the freedoms of the French Revolution. In one European country after another —throughout Italy, Switzerland, Holland, Belgium, Poland, Spain, and

much of Germany—Napoleon and his forces overthrew kings and nobles, uprooted the feudal system and gave oppressed peoples their first taste of the new liberty.

Although Napoleon was eventually defeated at the Battle of Waterloo in 1815, European life never again returned to what it had been before the French Revolution. True, most of the former kings regained their thrones, but many of the freedoms which the French had introduced remained. The feudal system was forever gone from western Europe and belief in freedom of religion, speech, and assembly was beginning to take root in European life.

What about the Jews? When Betty had finished reading about the French Revolution she couldn't help wondering what had been the effect of the ideas of "Liberty, Fraternity, Equality!" upon the lot of the European Jews. "Had they also benefited from the new freedoms?" she asked herself.

She turned to the second book that Great-Grandfather had left with her. It proved to be a history of the Jews, and it, too, contained a chapter on the French Revolution. She began reading once again.

Betty quickly discovered that despite the coming of the French Revolution, complete citizenship for the 50,000 Jews of France was not easily won. There were still many who wanted the Jews to remain under the old restrictions. While, prior to the Revolution, some of the Jews of Spanish descent enjoyed certain privileges in the southern part of France, French Jews of German ancestry, and particularly those in Alsace and Lorraine, suffered the same hardships as did the rest of European Jewry. Ghetto conditions and heavy taxes oppressed them, and because they were not part of the feudal system, they could earn their livelihood in only a limited number of occupations.

The Jews Finally Obtain Citizenship. With the outbreak of the Revolution in 1789, it seemed at first as if, instead of benefiting, the Jews would be among the chief victims. For even as the French mobs stormed the castles of the nobles, some turned against the Jews. In Alsace there was such wide-spread destruction of Jewish homes and property that hundreds of Jews were forced to flee the country. The peasants, it seems, blamed the Jews for their poverty but in reality the nobles and the feudal system were the real cause.

Gradually, as the National Assembly restored order in France, the persecution of Jews died down. On August 4, 1789, Jewish hopes for freedom were aroused when the National Assembly approved the principle of equality for all citizens, and, nineteen days later, passed a law guaranteeing all Frenchmen religious freedom. Immediately Jewish

representatives petitioned the National Assembly for full citizenship for French Jewry. However, fearing the outbreak of riots against Jews in those sections of France where they had always been persecuted, the Assembly postponed its decision. But it did grant citizenship to those Jews of Spanish descent who lived in southern France.

Meanwhile, the Jews were not without powerful friends in the Assembly. One was Count Mirabeau, a prominent leader of the Revolution and an ardent admirer of Moses Mendelssohn. Some years before, he had stated, "If we want the Jews to become useful citizens, then we must banish humiliating restrictions that we have placed upon them."

Another of their champions was the Abbé Gregoire, a noted Catholic priest and revolutionary figure. He constantly agitated for their freedom and in their behalf wrote the widely-circulated pamphlet, "Proposals in Favor of the Jews." Count Clermont-Tonnerre, also a member of the National Assembly, called upon the delegates to grant Jews immediate citizenship as atonement for the many sins that had been committed against them in the past.

Other delegates joined with these in pleading the cause of the Jews, but the Assembly delayed the final decision. It did, however, recognize the important military and financial service that Jews had rendered the Revolution by officially relieving French

Jewry of all special taxation. Finally, on September 27, 1791, after the repeated call of the delegates for action, the National Assembly proclaimed all Jews of France full citizens.

Thus, more than two years after the beginning of the Revolution, French Jewry finally received its freedom. How the Jews rejoiced over their new-found liberties! A letter of Berr Isaac Berr, a prominent Jewish representative of Lorraine, tells of his feelings at receiving the news. "We have at last again obtained the rights of which we have been deprived for eighteen centuries," he wrote. "How deeply at this moment should we recognize the wonderful grace of the God of our forefathers!" And in gratitude the Jews of France outdid themselves in support of their country which was then in the midst of war. A great number promptly enlisted in the army, and practically all contributed funds to the cause. Even synagogue valuables were sold to raise money to support the struggle against France's enemies.

And, as the victorious armies of France marched through Europe, citizenship for the Jews was one of the many freedoms they instituted. At last the Jews of Holland, Belgium, Italy, and many portions of Germany were released from the ghetto and emancipated. In other sections of Europe the example of France compelled the kings to extend greater rights to their oppressed Jews.

Napoleon and the Jews. But suddenly the Jews of France found their newly-won liberties endangered. Napoleon Bonaparte, leader of the French armies and soon to be the Emperor of France, received evil reports about the Jews. He was falsely led to believe that Jewish moneylenders were robbing the French people. He promised the enemies of the Jews in Alsace that he would take action against them, and upon the advice of a prejudiced counselor, he decided to deprive French Jewry of its citizenship.

Fortunately a number of prominent Frenchmen came to their defense and pleaded with him not to turn against the Jews. In an attempt to appear fair, Napoleon invited Jewish representatives from France, Germany, and Italy to meet in Paris as an Assembly of Jewish Notables. The purpose of the meeting, he stated, was to "create useful citizens of the Jews and to give them an opportunity to answer the charges that had been made against them." In reality, however, Napoleon planned to use this Assembly as a means of restricting Jewish freedom.

Questions and Answers. The 110 delegates to the Assembly of Jewish Notables met on July 26, 1806, and after electing officers, were asked by Napoleon to submit answers to twelve questions: (1) Are Jews permitted to have several wives? (2) Do Jews consider a Jewish divorce legal

Jews attending the Assembly of the Great Sanhedrin.

without the approval of the French courts? (3) According to Jewish law, may Jews intermarry with Christians? (4) Do the Jews of France regard all Frenchmen as their brothers? (5) What duties have Jews toward their fellow citizens? (6) Do French Jews look upon France as their country and do they feel obligated to obey its laws? (7) Who appoints the rabbis? (8) Do the rabbis have the right to enact laws for the Jews of France? (9) Is their power based upon the Written or Oral Laws of Judaism? (10) Are there any occupations forbidden to Jews? (11) Does Jewish law prohibit Jews from lending money at high rates of interest to fellow Jews? (12) Does it permit them to do so to non-Jews?

In less than a month the Assembly of Jewish Notables had agreed upon its reply. Napoleon was so pleased with the answers that he sent the following message to the delegates: "His Majesty guarantees you free practice of Judaism and full enjoyment of political rights."

To make certain that the answers given him were in agreement with Jewish law, Napoleon ordered the Jews to organize a special Sanhedrin to ratify the Assembly's decisions. Actually there had not been a meeting of a Sanhedrin, the highest Jewish court, since the days our people had lived in Palestine. Now, however, on February 9, 1807, a Great Sanhedrin convened in Paris. The seventy-one members, two-thirds of whom were rabbis, officially adopted the answers given by the Assembly of Jewish Notables.

In brief, they agreed that Judaism possessed two principal kinds of regulations. One was the religious commandments which must remain unchanged; the other was the political laws under which Jews had once lived in Palestine. Since no Jewish state was now in existence, these laws were no longer binding. Instead, Jews were subject to the laws of the lands in which they were living at the time.

The Sanhedrin proceeded to answer the other questions. It pointed out that for nearly 800 years Jewish law had prohibited Jews from having more than one wife. Moreover, it was agreed that Jews seeking to be married or divorced must first obtain legal permission under the laws of the countries in which they lived.

The statement of the Sanhedrin went on to declare that Jews loved their country, would happily serve in the armed forces to defend it, and regarded their non-Jewish fellow citizens as their brothers. It recommended that Jews should give up trading and money-lending for the more desirable occupations of farming and manufacturing.

Finally, in making its declaration on the issue of intermarriage, the Sanhedrin announced that while no rabbi could perform such a marriage, it would nonetheless be recognized as legal according to the laws of France.

Although Napoleon expressed his complete satisfaction with the response of the Assembly of Jewish Notables and Great Sanhedrin, he showed his real feelings by ordering the Jews of France to undergo a ten-year "training-period." For this purpose he issued special laws governing Jews and regulating their business activities. However, within a few years most of these restrictions had been removed in many sections of France, and when, after the ten-year period was over, the laws were not renewed, all of French Jewry enjoyed complete freedom.

It was the first time since the early days of the Roman Empire that the Jews of any European country possessed full and equal citizenship.

On to an Early Reform Temple. When Betty had finished the chapter, she looked up from her book, and to her surprise there was Great-Grandfather sitting across the room. He had come in so quietly that she hadn't even heard him.

"My," she said to Great-Grandfather, "that was some revolution!"

Great-Grandfather nodded in agreement. Then he asked her, "How do you suppose the emancipation of the Jews would affect the Judaism of the ghetto?"

Betty thought a moment. "I guess the old Judaism would have to change." She stopped, then added, "In fact, didn't the Great Sanhedrin admit that the political laws that had once regulated Jewish life were no longer binding?"

"That's right."

"Well, I imagine that this would be the beginning of other changes in Judaism. . . ."

"Yes, yes?" Great-Grandfather urged her.

"Of course," Betty shouted jubilantly, "this is the start of Reform Judaism!"

Betty could see from Great-Grandfather's pleased expression that she was on the right track.

"Now what happened?" she questioned him. "Where do we go from here?"

"Why, to one of the first Reform temples, of course," he replied.

1. Why do many people regard "modern times" as beginning with the French Revolution?

2. How do the causes which led to the French Revolution differ from those that gave rise to the American Revolution?

3. What was the importance of the French Revolution to the European Jew?

4. In what ways would the French Revolution affect the Judaism of the ghetto?

5. How did the statements of the Assembly of Jewish Notables and Great Sanhedrin contribute to the development of Reform Judaism?

6. On the basis of Jewish practice today what answers could be given to the various questions that Napoleon asked of the Assembly of Jewish Notables and Great Sanhedrin?

1. Let the class act as a "Great Sanhedrin." Prepare answers which would be suitable today to the questions that Napoleon asked of the original Great Sanhedrin. Compare your answers with those given to Napoleon.

2. Prepare a "March of Time" broadcast on the subject: "The French Revolution and the Jews."

3. Construct a map of Europe showing those areas in which Jews came to receive their freedom as a result of the French Revolution and Napoleon.

FEUER, LEON I. and AZRIEL EISENBERG, *Jewish Literature Since the Bible, II,* pp. 161-163.

GOLUB, JACOB S. and ALAN S. GREEN, *A Short History of the Jews, III,* pp. 9-12.

SOLOFF, MORDECAI I., *How the Jewish People Lives Today,* pp. 124-137.

References for the Teacher

Encyclopedia Britannica, "France," Vol. 9, pp. 634-645.

GRAETZ, HEINRICH, *History of the Jews,* "The French Revolution and the Emancipation of the Jews," Vol. 5, Chap. 11; "The Jewish-French Synhedrion and the Jewish Consistories," Vol. 5, Chap. 12.

Jewish Encyclopedia, "France," Vol. 5, pp. 467-470; "Napoleon Bonaparte," Vol. 9, pp. 167-168.

SACHAR, ABRAM L., *A History of the Jews,* Chap. 21, "The Fall of the Medieval Citadel."

SCHWARTZMAN, SYLVAN D., *Reform Judaism in the Making,* Chap. 4, "The European Jew Becomes a Citizen."

Universal Jewish Encyclopedia, "France," Vol. 4, pp. 376-378; "Napoleon Bonaparte," Vol. 8, pp. 100-101.

5. BETTY GOES TO THE HAMBURG TEMPLE

Changes and More Changes. Great-Grandfather cleared his throat. He was ready to tell Betty about the beginnings of the Reform movement, but he could see that she was occupied with thoughts of her own.

As a matter of fact, Betty was reviewing in her mind the experience of European Jewry. She recalled the hardships of the ghetto—how Jews were forced to live by themselves, compelled to wear yellow badges and pay special taxes. She remembered, too, how they were barred from many occupations and how they lived in fear of sudden attack by their enemies.

But she didn't overlook the more satisfying side of ghetto life. After all, living together in one area did give the Jews of the ghetto a greater sense of security against attack and there, too, they were free to direct their own community affairs. There were other advantages as well—a

more wholesome family life, better education, uniform Jewish observance, and the promise of future rewards as compensation for suffering.

At this point, Betty couldn't help wondering about the effects of the French Revolution upon this type of Jewish life. Now that Jews fully participated in the political life of their countries, would there still be need for separate self-governing community organization? When German Jews, for example, mingled freely with their fellow citizens, would they continue to speak their own Judeo-German language? And once the people became familiar with the culture of the outside world, wouldn't Jewish boys and girls study European history, science and thought?

And above all, Betty questioned whether the modern Jew could abide by all the regulations of the old Judaism. As long as ghetto conditions prevailed, it hadn't mattered that Jewish law remained practically unchanged for centuries. But now that the people were emancipated, it seemed that many of those laws could no longer be observed. Even the Great Sanhedrin, she reminded herself, admitted this. Wasn't it natural, therefore, that other Jewish practices should be modified to fit the new conditions of Jewish citizenship?

Great-Grandfather waited very patiently for Betty to pay attention. Finally she looked up and he started to speak. He first told her about a group of Moses Mendelssohn's friends who, as early as 1783, had begun to prepare ghetto Jewry for participation in European life. They published a magazine called *The Gatherer* in which they proposed suggestions for meeting some of the problems about which Betty had just been thinking. Great-Grandfather then told Betty about the Adath Jeshurun Congregation of Amsterdam which in 1796 had introduced a few modifications of the prayer book and Jewish burial customs.

As he went on speaking, Betty felt herself growing drowsy. She leaned back and shut her eyes. Great-Grandfather's voice seemed to be coming to her from way off in a distance. . . .

Betty Drops in at Temple. Suddenly Betty found herself in the city of Hamburg. As she passed through the narrow streets, she came upon a crowd making its way into what appeared to be a new building. It was obvious that this was the Hamburg Temple, and she followed the crowd through the main door.

When Betty got inside she took a quick look around. "This couldn't be a Reform temple," she told herself, for it looked to her just like the Orthodox synagogue that she and Mildred had attended. The women were seated in a separate section, and all the men wore hats and talesim. There was the pulpit in the center of the synagogue in addition to the one up front. Yet the tablet on the wall told her that this was indeed the Hamburg Temple, dedicated on October 18, 1818.

Betty took one of the prayer books and found herself a seat in the women's section. Soon the service commenced. She was greatly pleased to hear the organ and choir accompany the congregation in the opening hymn, and she noted that everyone sang in German.

The service was conducted mainly in Hebrew, but there were also some prayers in German. She observed, too, that a few of the Hebrew passages were different from those that were recited in the shul. When the time for the sermon arrived, a distinguished-looking man came to the pulpit and delivered an address in German. The service was concluded with several Hebrew and German prayers and a final hymn.

Rabbi Kley Greets Betty. As Betty rose to leave, the man who had given the sermon came over and greeted her.

"Good Shabos," he said. "I'm Rabbi Edward Kley. We're very happy to have you with us."

"Good Shabos," responded Betty. "I'm Betty Friedberg."

"I noticed that you were looking around during the service. Is there anything that you would like explained?" he asked. "Our congregation is Reform, you know."

Betty came right to the point. "Tell me," she asked bluntly, "what's Reform about it?" She saw that Rabbi Kley was taken aback by her question.

"Didn't you notice any differences?" he asked in surprise. "We use the organ and recite our prayers in German as well as Hebrew. You heard the sermon in German, too, and you surely couldn't miss some of the revisions that we've made in the prayers. For example, we have no prayers for the coming of a Messiah to deliver us because we don't consider ourselves in exile any longer."

"Yes," Betty admitted, "I agree that your service is somewhat different from the Orthodox, but you haven't advanced very far beyond it."

"Don't imagine that even the limited progress we've made has been easy," cautioned Rabbi Kley. "We've had to face the continuous opposition of the three Orthodox rabbis of Hamburg. They've repeatedly urged the Senate to close our temple. They've circulated letters to all the important rabbis of Europe warning them about us and published the replies which condemn us as 'sinful people' and 'traitors to Judaism.' Fortunately, the president of our congregation has received support from other rabbis commending our actions, and a well-known Hungarian rabbi has defended our reforms with proof from the Talmud itself."

"But why do the Orthodox rabbis object so strongly to your temple?" Betty wanted to know.

"They regard us as sinners because we have dared to make changes in Jewish worship. They insist that the only way of worship for the Jew is the Orthodox, for they say that it was God Himself who established it that way and only He can change it. Therefore, anyone who introduces changes in the service is guilty of violating God's commandments."

"But actually yours are such small changes. . . ."

"They're afraid that these minor changes may lead to others more far-reaching. But," he went on, "they are mistaken in their understanding of Judaism. Even the Talmud itself gives us the authority for introducing our present reforms. What's more, how can they expect Judaism to survive unless it meets the religious needs of modern Jews? Should we be forever denied the inspiration of organ music in our worship because many centuries ago it was forbidden by Jewish law? May we not pray in the language we speak, especially when Hebrew is no longer understood by many of our people?"

Betty was impressed by his arguments and felt that he was right. Surely, if the Jewish religion were to prosper, it must be permitted to change from its ghetto forms.

Israel Jacobson Begins Reform. Beckoning to a well-dressed gentleman who stood nearby, Rabbi Kley turned to Betty and said, "Now I should like you to meet the individual who really started the Reform movement, the well-known businessman, Israel Jacobson." Israel Jacobson bowed.

Betty acknowledged the introduction and then said to Mr. Jacobson, "I'm very curious. Tell me, how does

Israel Jacobson

it happen that a layman, rather than a rabbi, started Reform Judaism?"

"It was sort of an accident," Israel Jacobson admitted. "It all began with a new Jewish school that we organized at Seesen, a small town about seventy-five miles south of Hanover in Germany. Even before we began to receive political rights, some of us felt that we were not fully prepared to take our place in German life. While most of us received a thorough Hebrew education, we learned very little about general history, geography, and German literature. Many of us couldn't even read or speak good German. Yet, we reasoned that if we were to become useful citizens, then we ought to study these subjects, too.

"And so," Mr. Jacobson continued, "we supported a movement to establish a new type of Jewish school in which our boys and girls could study both Jewish and German subjects. In 1778, David Friedländer, a good friend of Moses Mendelssohn, organized the Jewish Free School in Berlin, and soon there were several such institutions in Germany. I started a school, too, at Seesen, and there we conducted regular Sabbath services for the students. Because I was anxious that the students should enjoy their worship, we included prayers in the German language and the singing of German as well as Hebrew hymns. Each week we would invite a guest preacher to deliver the sermon in German, and the regular weekly sermon became part of our

Sabbath service. In most Orthodox synagogues, you see, the rabbis delivered only two or three sermons a year—one before Passover, one during the High Holydays, and sometimes another on Yom Kippur eve—and these dealt chiefly with interpretation of the laws of these holidays. Furthermore, these were rarely delivered in the language of the country in which the Jews lived."

Reform Moves to Berlin. Israel Jacobson went on. "But I must tell you frankly that one of the strongest reasons that persuaded me to start a movement for reforms in Judaism was the fact that so many Jews were converting to Christianity. They were not happy with Orthodoxy and yet no other form of Judaism was available to them. I soon realized that it was necessary to develop a Judaism that was Jewish in every sense of the word and, at the same time, a religion which would command the respect of Jews and non-Jews.

"Many of my own Jewish friends told me of their dissatisfaction with the unattractiveness of synagogue services. They had difficulty in following the all-Hebrew prayers and were ashamed of the noise and confusion that went on during the service. Consequently, I invited some of them to worship with our students at Seesen and they so thoroughly enjoyed our services that many of them attended every Sabbath. They wel-

comed the order and dignity of the worship and the many prayers recited in a language which they could understand.

"When the French freed the Jews of Westphalia and put me in charge of Jewish affairs there, I established another school at Cassell. Here in 1810 I introduced the new ceremony of Confirmation, the consecration of Jewish boys and girls to their religion, and this was the first time girls were permitted to participate in a synagogue ritual."

Rabbi Kley broke in. "How well I remember that first Confirmation," he said. "It was conducted on the Sabbath immediately after the Torah reading. One of the students arose and recited the fundamental truths of Judaism. He then promised to remain forever faithful to his religion and loyal to his country. The ceremony was concluded when Rabbi Loeb Berlin, Chief-Rabbi of Westphalia, pronounced a special blessing upon him. It was a very stirring experience."

Mr. Jacobson was touched by his friend's comment and he remained silent until Rabbi Kley urged him to go on with his story. "Shortly after," Israel Jacobson said, "in the same year of 1810, I constructed a new synagogue at Seesen which became Europe's first Reform temple. There we provided a portable organ and a well-trained school choir. Soon a number of Jewish men and women in the neighborhood started worshipping with us every Sabbath morning.

"Then, in 1812, when the Jews of Prussia were liberated, I moved to Berlin and beginning in 1815, I conducted weekly Reform services for adults in my home. They were very much like the one you attended here in the Hamburg Temple, and were they popular! So many people came that we had to hold a second service in the home of Jacob Herz Beer, a wealthy Berlin banker. Rabbi Kley," he added, pointing to his friend, "served there as one of the preachers."

"This new type of service attracted such a large following," Rabbi Kley commented, "that we were planning to build a Reform temple in Berlin."

"Did you?" asked Betty.

Israel Jacobson answered her question. "No," he said sadly, "the Orthodox rabbis of Berlin and their followers, claiming to speak for the great majority of the Jewish community, condemned our services as 'sinful' and in 1817 called upon the government to put a stop to them. Six years later, as a result of their continued opposition, the king of Prussia prohibited all Jewish worship that was not strictly Orthodox. 'Henceforth,' his decree stated, 'Jewish services must not contain changes in language, ceremony, prayer, or song.' Thus Reform worship in Berlin had to cease."

"The king, you see, was opposed to all change in general. He consid-ered it dangerous," Rabbi Kley explained to Betty. "Just as he was afraid of changes in government, so he objected to reforms in religion. Furthermore, he believed that by preventing Judaism from adjusting to modern conditions he could cause Jews to become more and more dissatisfied with their religion and turn instead to Christianity."

"He was right, too," Israel Jacobson reminded his friend. "If you remember, after our Berlin services ceased, a number of Jews did become converted. Had Reform Judaism been allowed to continue, this might never have happened. They would certainly have seen that Judaism could be made meaningful and inspiring to modern Jews."

Hamburg Gets a Temple. "I suppose after that Reform services were transferred to Hamburg?" Betty asked.

"Yes," replied Rabbi Kley. "When I became the director of the Jewish Free School of Hamburg, I helped organize a society of Jews interested in Reform services. Then, in 1818, our group built this temple. What's more, we've started a branch temple at Leipzig where the yearly fairs are held, and merchants from all over Europe often attend the services. In this way they carry the new ideas of Reform back to their own communities."

"I'll make a prediction," ventured Israel Jacobson, "that it will not be too many years before Reform services will be conducted all over Europe. . . ."

"And in America, too," Betty chimed in knowingly.

Betty Returns Home. That was the last thing Betty remembered of her visit to the Hamburg Temple. Rabbi Kley and Mr. Jacobson vanished; the inside of the temple faded away. Betty blinked and opened her eyes. She was back in the living-room with Great-Grandfather.

"Do you know what Israel Jacobson just told me?" she asked him.

"Israel Jacobson!" he exclaimed in astonishment. "When did you ever speak with him?"

"When I visited the Hamburg Temple, of course," she replied.

Great-Grandfather looked at her queerly. "You must have been day-dreaming. Israel Jacobson has been dead since 1828."

"What!" shouted Betty. "Do you mean I dreamed all that?" And then in a quiet voice she said, "It was all so real. . . ."

"Well, tell me anyway how your dream finally turned out."

"Reform Judaism was growing stronger. Mr. Jacobson believed that there would soon be Reform congregations all over Europe."

"He was right about that," Great-Grandfather asserted. "A few years later there were Reform temples in Germany, Austria, France, and Denmark." He paused a moment. "But

didn't Israel Jacobson tell you about the new troubles that were brewing?" he asked.

"No," Betty shook her head. "When I left things were working out fine."

"Well, that didn't last long. Reform suddenly found itself with a real fight on its hands . . . a fight for its very survival!"

QUESTIONS FOR DISCUSSION

1. Why did Reform Judaism become a necessity after the French Revolution?
2. Why did the Orthodox and some governments oppose the introduction of reforms in Judaism?
3. How do the practices of the Hamburg Temple compare with those of your temple today?
4. What was the significance of the Hamburg Temple in the development of the Reform movement?
5. What motives prompted Israel Jacobson to begin the Reform movement?
6. In what ways does present-day Reform reflect the activities of Israel Jacobson?

SUGGESTED ACTIVITIES

1. Write and present a radio drama of the life of Israel Jacobson.
2. Conduct a debate in class between those representing Edward Kley and his supporters and those representing Orthodox opponents of Reform in Hamburg.

3. Create a newspaper article dealing with the founding of the Hamburg Temple.

ADDITIONAL READINGS FOR PUPILS

FEUER, LEON I. and AZRIEL EISENBERG, *Jewish Literature Since the Bible, II,* pp. 181-182.

GOLUB, JACOB S. and ALAN S. GREEN, *A Short History of the Jews, III,* p. 18.

LEVINGER, LEE J., *A History of the Jews in the United States,* p. 212.

SOLOFF, MORDECAI I., *How the Jewish People Lives Today,* pp. 138-142.

References for the Teacher

GRAETZ, HEINRICH, *History of the Jews,* "Reform and Young Israel," Vol. 5, Chap. 15.

Jewish Encyclopedia, "Israel Jacobson," Vol. 7, p. 47; "Israel (Edward) Kley," Vol. 7, p. 524.

MARCUS, JACOB R., *Central Conference of American Rabbis Yearbook,* "Israel Jacobson, An Appraisal," Vol. 38, pp. 386-481.

PHILIPSON, DAVID, *The Reform Movement in Judaism,* pp. 11-18 (Israel Jacobson); pp. 21-38 (early reforms and Hamburg Temple).

SCHWARTZMAN, SYLVAN D., *Reform Judaism in the Making,* Chap. 5, "The Beginnings of Reform."

Universal Jewish Encyclopedia, "Israel Jacobson," Vol. 6, p. 22; "Israel Kley (Edward Kley)," Vol. 6, p. 418.

6. "DOWN WITH REFORM!"

Reform Faces a Fight for Existence. "Yes," Great-Grandfather repeated, "only ten years after Israel Jacobson's death Reform faced a fight for its very existence."

"Was it the kings again this time?" Betty questioned.

"Yes, partly. But the Orthodox rabbis and their followers were just as much to blame. . . ."

"I still can't understand why they insisted on fighting the Reformers," Betty blurted out. "After all, the Orthodox had their own synagogues in which they could do as they pleased. Why couldn't they allow the Reform group to worship as they wanted to in their own temples—just as we have it today?"

"In those days," Great-Grandfather explained, "it was natural for the Orthodox to think of all Jews as identified with only one form of Judaism—their own. After all, this had been true for many centuries, and it was difficult for the leaders of Orthodoxy to realize that times had changed. Therefore, they regarded the Reform movement as something unheard of, a threat to the Jewish religion, by which they meant, of course, their own beliefs and practices."

"I begin to see," said Betty. "The whole idea of different groups within Judaism was something they weren't used to."

"Yes, but that was only part of Orthodoxy's objection to Reform," Great-Grandfather declared. "You'll soon see that there was much more involved." He paused a moment and then asked Betty to hand him the scrap-book which was lying on the mantel.

Betty rose and took down the large scrap-book. "Look over some of the clippings," Great-Grandfather called out to her, "and I believe you'll understand why the Reform movement faced such a bitter struggle for its existence. . . ."

Geiger-Tiktin Affair, 1838–1844. She opened the scrap-book and glanced over the old news clippings pasted there. On one of the pages there were three which interested her and she read them carefully.

RABBI ABRAHAM GEIGER ELECTED TO SERVE BRESLAU CONGREGATION

Reform Leader Becomes Associate of Breslau Chief-Rabbi; Chief-Rabbi S. A. Tiktin a Noted Supporter of Orthodoxy

BRESLAU, July 26, 1838—Dr. Abraham Geiger, well-known Reform rabbi of Germany, was elected today by the Breslau congregation to serve as associate to Rabbi S. A. Tiktin, Orthodox Chief-Rabbi of the community. Rabbi Geiger was chosen by a vote of 56-1.

Dr. Geiger has served as spiritual leader of the Wiesbaden community for the past six years, and although only twenty-eight years of age, he is a university graduate with a doctor's degree received in 1833. Thoroughly learned in Judaism, he has been a leader in the movement to study Jewish history scientifically in an effort to discover ways in which Judaism may be modified to meet modern conditions. In 1835 he founded a special magazine for this purpose.

The present Chief-Rabbi of Breslau, S. A. Tiktin, has been with the congregation since 1821 and has consistently opposed all changes from strict Orthodox practice. He has frequently led protests against reforms of Jewish worship and observance.

Prior to the selection of Rabbi Geiger, many members of the Breslau congregation had urged the appointment of a spiritual leader trained along more modern lines, and sought a rabbi who would introduce religious reforms. Dr. Geiger met with their approval since, in his trial sermon and in many of his writings, he advocated the adjustment of Judaism to the needs of the times. However, he has insisted that all such changes should be approved by a special rabbinical conference called for the purpose.

The new rabbi will preach a weekly sermon in German and take charge of instructing the young people.

DR. GEIGER WINS FIRST FIGHT; OBTAINS PRUSSIAN CITIZENSHIP

Orthodox Faction Led by Chief-Rabbi Loses Legal Battle; Geiger Gains Right to Serve Breslau Jewish Congregation

BRESLAU, Dec. 6, 1839—Dr. Abraham Geiger, newly elected rabbinical colleague of Rabbi S. A. Tiktin, today won his fight for Prussian citizenship against his Breslau Orthodox opponents. Geiger's replies to their charges were

Abraham Geiger

declared satisfactory by Prussian government officials and he has been granted final papers entitling him to full rights of citizenship.

The Orthodox group which opposes all reforms of Judaism had sought to bar him from occupying the Breslau post. According to law, Dr. Geiger, who was born in Frankfort and hence was not a Prussian citizen, was not eligible to serve in Breslau. He therefore put in his application for citizenship in the Prussian state.

Four members of the congregation representing the Orthodox faction petitioned the Prussian officials to deny his request. They claimed that Rabbi Geiger was compelled to leave his previous post at Wiesbaden because he had violated the Sabbath. They also contended that the election by which he became rabbi of the Breslau congregation was improperly conducted and that he was ineligible for the position because his religious views were unacceptable to the Orthodox membership.

However, the government today overruled their objections, and Dr. Abraham Geiger's victory represents a major defeat for the Breslau Orthodox opposition.

Immediately following the announcement of the Prussian government's decision, the Breslau Reform congregation declared that Rabbi Geiger would deliver his inaugural sermon on January 4, 1840.

GEIGER-TIKTIN STRUGGLE ENDED; REFORM WINS COMPLETE VICTORY

Geiger Given Post of Chief-Rabbi after Tiktin's Death; Orthodox Forbidden by Government to Leave Congregation

BRESLAU, Oct. 26, 1844—The threat of the Orthodox membership to resign from the Breslau congregation should Dr. Abraham Geiger succeed the late Rabbi S. A. Tiktin as Chief-Rabbi was withdrawn today as a result of a government order.

Government officials confirmed Dr. Geiger's election as Chief-Rabbi and proposed the selection of a second rabbi to serve with him. The government furthermore warned the Orthodox opposition not to withdraw from the congregation.

This latest action ends the Geiger-Tiktin feud which has raged ever since Dr. Geiger was elected as associate of Rabbi Tiktin six years ago.

During the opening struggle between the Orthodox and Reform factions, the former succeeded in delaying Rabbi Geiger's appointment for more than seventeen months while they contested his right to Prussian citizenship. But Geiger was finally granted his citizenship.

However, Rabbi Tiktin refused to recognize him as his rabbinical colleague when Geiger stated in his inaugural sermon, "Judaism is not a finished tale; there is much in its present form that must be changed or abolished." At the time Tiktin said that his opposition to Geiger was prompted by his desire to protect Judaism. "The safety of Judaism," he declared in a public statement, "is involved in any single change, since all of its laws and practices are sacred."

Nevertheless, Dr. Geiger carried on his congregational activities—preaching weekly sermons in German, conducting classes for the young, lecturing and writing in behalf of reforms in Judaism. But Rabbi Tiktin continued the fight against him. "Judaism," Tiktin vigorously contended, "permits no criticism of its sacred teachings. Anyone who disobeys a single commandment is no Jew!"

The officers of the congregation tried in vain to end the hostility between its rabbis. It offered a compromise plan similar to one followed in Vienna and Prague which would have made Tiktin the rabbi and Geiger the preacher. The plan was not acceptable to Dr. Geiger, however, because he believed it would divide the congregation as well as give Tiktin the authority to stifle all reforms.

Shortly thereafter, Tiktin's continued antagonism compelled the congregation to suspend him from office. He appealed for support to his Orthodox colleagues of Europe and in June of 1842 he had their statements published. They agreed that the commandments of Judaism could be changed only by God and that those guilty of altering Judaism in any way could not be considered Jews.

In self-defense the congregational governing board who supported Geiger's program appealed to the more liberal European rabbis for their opinions. The two volumes of replies, published in 1842 and 1843, confirmed the fact that Judaism could be modified, especially in view of the changed circumstances of the times. They pointed out that throughout history the Jewish religion had undergone constant change in the course of its development. Just as the rabbis of the Talmud were free to reinterpret some of the older practices of the Bible, so now rabbis might modify Jewish observances to meet modern conditions. Moreover, such reforms would not only encourage Jews to remain faithful to their religion; they would also stimulate new religious interest and creativity.

But the Reform group suffered a setback when the government declared Rabbi Tiktin's suspension from office illegal and ordered him restored to his rabbinical post.

Tiktin's death in March of last year temporarily halted the struggle between the Orthodox and Reform elements. However, when it seemed certain that Geiger would be elected Chief-Rabbi, the Orthodox, under the leadership of Rabbi Tiktin's son, decided to withdraw and form their own congregation.

The government's order today thus ends the fight which has raged in Breslau throughout the past six years and which attracted the attention of Jews all over the world. It represents a complete triumph for the Reform movement.

The Hamburg Prayer Book Controversy. Betty skipped several pages until she came across the following clipping:

TEMPLE PRAYER BOOK DENOUNCED BY HAMBURG ORTHODOX COMMUNITY

Revised Temple Prayer Book Arouses Orthodox Hostility; Chief-Rabbi Issues Second Warning against Reform Liturgy

HAMBURG, Dec. 1, 1842—The Hamburg Temple now finds itself the center of the fiercest fight since its founding in 1818. This latest struggle between Orthodox and Reform camps originated last year with the publication of the temple's newly revised prayer book.

Until the prayer book issue arose the Jewish community of Hamburg enjoyed peaceful relations between its Reform and Orthodox elements.

Over the past years the rapid growth of membership which prompted the Reform temple to enlarge its house of worship also produced a shortage of prayer books. The preparation of a new edition of the temple's prayer book was proposed by the congregation in 1839 and a committee of two rabbis and three laymen was appointed.

The new edition which was published last year differed only slightly from the old. While prayers for the rebuilding of Zion were retained, others calling for the coming of the Messiah and the deliverance of all Jews from exile were again omitted.

Immediately upon its appearance, Rabbi Isaac Bernays, Chief-Rabbi of the Hamburg community and spokesman for the Orthodox group, denounced it. On October 16, 1841, he issued a public warning forbidding the use of the temple prayer book. "Any Jew worshipping with it," he cautioned, "is not fulfilling his Jewish obligations."

Temple officials promptly took issue with him. While expressing regret that the Chief-Rabbi had seen fit to stir up friction within the community, the Reform group declared that he had no authority over them.

Even though the Hamburg Senate compelled the Chief-Rabbi to withdraw his warning on January 12 of this year, Rabbi Isaac Bernays has renewed his prohibition against the temple prayer book.

The directors of the temple have appealed to leading European rabbis to present their opinions of the new prayer book. To date twelve replies have been received. In general, they condemn the narrow attitude of the Chief-Rabbi and his Orthodox followers, and declare the prayer book to be thoroughly Jewish in content and completely acceptable for congregational worship.

Reform Comes to England. The last clipping that Betty read was:

ORTHODOX REFUSE RECOGNITION TO NEW LONDON REFORM TEMPLE

Religious Ban Proclaimed against London Reform Members; Chief-Rabbi Refuses to Wed Orthodox Man to Reform Girl

LONDON, March 3, 1846—The struggle of London's Orthodox Jews against Reform grew more intense tonight when Chief-Rabbi Nathan M. Adler announced that he had refused to perform the marriage of an Orthodox man to a young lady whose father was a temple member unless she promised never again to set foot in the Reform synagogue.

This latest incident climaxes a series of events which began six years ago when, on April 15, 1840, twenty-four members of the German and Portuguese synagogues formed the "West London Synagogue of British Jews." According to the declaration of the founders, the new Reform congregation planned to shorten the services, remove certain outmoded prayers, provide more convenient hours of worship, and introduce an English sermon into the service.

As far back as 1824 certain members of the Portuguese synagogue had objected to the noise and disturbances during worship, and in 1836 some members petitioned the congregational governing board to introduce the more modern service of the Hamburg Temple.

In protest the Orthodox immediately issued a counter-petition opposing even the most minor reforms, and their position was upheld by the officials of the congregation.

Seven years ago Reform members again petitioned the synagogue officials for a shorter service at a more convenient time, a choir, English sermons, and elimination of the extra days of the Jewish holidays. Once again their request was denied.

Permission was then sought by the Reformers to establish a branch synagogue near their homes in the West End of London, but it was not granted. A compromise proposed by the Orthodox that a branch synagogue be permitted if it retain complete Orthodox observance was rejected by the Reform group. "We are acting to preserve Judaism for our children," the Reform leaders stated. "We want to prevent Jews from leaving Judaism." They then organized the independent "West London Synagogue of British Jews."

Five days before the new Reform temple was dedicated the London Orthodox rabbis issued a stern warning that the use of the Reform prayer book was a serious violation of Jewish law. Later they forbade Orthodox Jews from participating in Reform religious ceremonies and declared Reform members ineligible to participate in Jewish community life.

Thus, when officials of the Reform congregation applied to the Board of Deputies of British Jews—the supreme authority over Jewish affairs in England—to empower their rabbi to perform legally-recognized Jewish marriages, their request was promptly refused. To date the Orthodox still dispute the right of a Reform rabbi to perform a Jewish marriage in England.

The Chief-Rabbi's refusal tonight to officiate at the wedding of an Orthodox and a Reform Jew further aggravates the strained relations that divide the Jewish community of London.

Reform Has Its Own Troubles, Too. When Betty had finished she looked up at Great-Grandfather. "Reform Jews didn't have an easy time of it in those days, did they?"

"Hardly," he answered, "but we had no choice. We had to fight for the right to modernize our religion." Great-Grandfather took the scrapbook and thumbed through it as he spoke. He stopped at one page and held the book open for Betty. "This should interest you," he said. "It's a letter more than a hundred years old addressed to your great-great-grandfather."

Betty came over and looked. This is what she saw:

April 3, 1844

Mr. Jacob Friedberg
14 Hertzen Place
Frankfort-on-the-Main, Germany
Honored Sir:

As President of your congregation, you will be interested to know of the coming Rabbinical Conference to be held in Brunswick from June 12th through 19th of this year.

Since we are planning to discuss the principles of Judaism in an effort to decide upon changes that will modernize our faith, it is important that your rabbi be present.

I shall deeply appreciate it if you would kindly urge your rabbi to attend.

Most respectfully yours,
(Signed) *Abraham Geiger*

Betty put down the scrap-book. "Why was it necessary to have a rabbinical conference make the changes in Judaism?" she asked. "Weren't various temples already introducing reforms of their own?"

"That was Reform's difficulty."

"I thought the only Reform difficulties were those caused by the Orthodox," commented Betty.

"Oh, no," Great-Grandfather answered, "Reform was having plenty of troubles of its own, too."

"For example?" Betty asked.

"Well," began Great-Grandfather as he started to explain. . . .

QUESTIONS FOR DISCUSSION

1. What were some of the factors which led to the conflict between Rabbis Geiger and Tiktin?
2. What was the significance of the Geiger-Tiktin controversy for the development of Reform?
3. Of what consequence to the Reform movement was the Hamburg prayer book controversy?
4. How did Reform begin in England?
5. What measures did the Orthodox take to prevent the growth of Reform in England?
6. What are the basic attitudes of the early Reformers and their opponents which are revealed through the various controversies that took place?

SUGGESTED ACTIVITIES

1. Construct a map of Europe showing the important Reform developments from the movement's beginning.
2. Let some members of the class become the Board of Deputies of British Jews to hear and discuss the appeal of others representing London Reform Jews who have come to ask that their rabbi be empowered to perform marriages.
3. Prepare a pamphlet dealing with the early history of your temple and some of the problems which the young congregation faced.

ADDITIONAL READINGS FOR PUPILS

FEUER, LEON I. and AZRIEL EISENBERG, *Jewish Literature Since the Bible, II,* pp. 183-186.

GOLUB, JACOB S. and ALAN S. GREEN, *A Short History of the Jews, III,* pp. 18-19.

LEVINGER, LEE J., *A History of the Jews in the United States,* pp. 210-213.

SOLOFF, MORDECAI I., *How the Jewish People Lives Today,* pp. 143-149.

References for the Teacher

Jewish Encyclopedia, "Isaac Bernays," Vol. 3, pp. 90-91; "Abraham Geiger," Vol. 5, pp. 584-587.

PHILIPSON, DAVID, *Central Conference of American Rabbis Yearbook,* "Geiger the Reformer," Vol. 20, pp. 246-283.

——, *The Reform Movement in Judaism,* Chap. 3, "The Geiger-Tiktin Affair"; Chap. 4, "The Hamburg Temple Prayer Book Controversy"; Chap. 5, "Reform in England."

SCHWARTZMAN, SYLVAN D., *Reform Judaism in the Making,* Chap. 6, "Reform Meets Major Opposition."

Universal Jewish Encyclopedia, "Isaac Bernays," Vol. 2, p. 226; "Abraham Geiger," Vol. 4, pp. 521-522.

7. GREAT-GRAND-FATHER POSES THE PROBLEMS

Mother and Father Join Betty. Great-Grandfather was just on the verge of describing the new difficulties that arose in Reform ranks when suddenly Mother called out from the kitchen.

"Supper's ready!"

Betty had been so absorbed in the story of the Reform movement that she hadn't noticed it growing dark outside. She and Great-Grandfather left together for the dining-room.

When they came in, Mother and Father were already seated at the table. "Hello," Betty called out. "Great-Grandfather's been telling me the story of Reform Judaism," she informed them as she took her place.

Father seemed a little surprised. "How did all this happen?"

"Well," Betty explained, "I went with Mildred to the Orthodox synagogue this morning, and I kept wondering why temple services were so different. When I got home I asked Great-Grandfather."

"And what's the answer?" Father asked.

"The story's not finished yet," replied Betty. "Great-Grandfather began with the 1700's when the Jews of Europe lived in ghettos and suffered all kinds of discrimination. Fortunately Judaism kept their hopes alive and encouraged them to develop strong Jewish community organization. After that we read parts of Great-Great-Grandfather's diary which told of Moses Mendelssohn's efforts to prepare Jews for their coming emancipation by encouraging them to learn the German language. At last, through the success of the French Revolution, all Jews were granted citizenship, and in order to adjust to their new circumstances some began making changes in the Orthodox forms of worship. Regular Reform services were soon held in Berlin and Hamburg, and gradually in many sections of Europe Reform temples were established. But don't think the Reformers had an easy time of it! They were under constant attack from the Orthodox who condemned every change."

EUROPEAN REFORM DEVELOPMENTS—TO 1815

Important Historical Events	Happenings in Jewish Life	Developments in European Reform
1776—Signing of the American Declaration of Independence		
		1778—Jewish Free School established in Berlin by Friedländer
	1779—Publication of Lessing's *Nathan the Wise*	
	1781—Dohm's plea for Jewish emancipation issued	
	1782—"Act of Tolerance" issued in Austria	
		1783—Completion of Mendelssohn's translation of the Five Books of Moses into German
1789—Outbreak of the French Revolution		
	1791—Granting of citizenship to French Jewry	
	1796—Granting of citizenship to the Jews of Holland	1796—Introduction of minor reforms in synagogue worship by Amsterdam congregation
1798—Establishment of the Roman and Swiss Republics		
		1801—Founding of the school at Seesen by Jacobson
1804—Napoleon crowned Emperor of France		
1806—Beginning of Napoleon's control of Germany	1806—Meeting of the Assembly of Jewish Notables	
	1807—Meeting of the Great Sanhedrin	
1808—Napoleon issues decree regulating the Jews of France	1808—Granting of citizenship to the Jews of Westphalia	1808—Establishment of a second school at Cassell by Jacobson
		1810—Building of the new synagogue at Seesen with use of an organ. First Confirmation held at Cassell
	1812—Prussian Jewry emancipated	
1815—Defeat of Napoleon at Waterloo		1815—Beginning of Reform services in Berlin

"I was just about to tell Betty of certain new Reform problems that began to appear," Great-Grandfather remarked.

"Sounds interesting," Mother commented. "I'd like to hear more."

"Me, too," seconded Father.

As soon as supper was over, the family gathered in the living-room. "All right," Mother reminded Great-Grandfather, "now you can tell us about those Reform problems."

Problem One: Reform Radicals. Great-Grandfather started speaking. "While the Orthodox were resisting the efforts to adjust Judaism to modern life," he began, "the Reform camp was threatened by a split. Some, known as 'radical Reformers,' were advocating violent changes in Judaism and they were being opposed by the more moderate Reform leaders who feared that such radical extremes would seriously endanger the Jewish religion. One of the best known of the radical groups was the Frankfort Reform Society. . . ."

"Don't you mean the 'Frankfort Reform *Congregation*'?" Mother questioned.

Great-Grandfather shook his head. "No," he answered, "during the early days of the movement Reform societies, instead of congregations, were organized in some of the leading cities. It was easier to get a Reform group started that way. Jews who were dissatisfied with Orthodox practices would get together to dis-

cuss religious changes and start conducting their own services. As a rule they were unable to secure a rabbi to lead them since most rabbis were Orthodox and would not serve groups that sought reforms. Later, many of these societies developed into congregations.

"The creation of the Reform Society of Frankfort was typical," he pointed out. "When the Orthodox rabbis put a stop to all religious change in the city's synagogues, Jews who desired a more modern form of worship held their own services in the local Jewish school where they introduced prayers in German, the weekly sermon, and special Confirmation exercises.

"Finally, in November of 1842, the group formed 'The Society of the Friends of Reform,' and the membership quickly grew to fifty. By August of the following year the Society issued a set of principles which it declared was necessary because of Orthodoxy's failure to recognize the changes that had taken place in Jewish life and to distinguish between the essential teachings of Judaism and some of its outmoded laws and ceremonies.

"These principles were three: (1) Judaism is not unchangeable; rather it is capable of developing and adjusting to new conditions. (2) Jews need no longer obey the laws of the Talmud. (3) Modern Jews no longer look forward to the coming of a Messiah who will lead them out of exile.

Instead, they regard the countries in which they dwell as their rightful and permanent homeland."

Father interrupted to ask, "What was so radical about these principles?"

"The noted Reform layman, Gabriel Riesser," Great-Grandfather disclosed, "condemned them as negative and a step backward because they offered no definite program for Reform but merely attacked Orthodox belief. Rabbi David Einhorn, another distinguished Reform spokesman, labeled the principles 'a confession of unbelief!'"

"I see," Father said. "In other words, they were too extreme."

"Yes," Great-Grandfather agreed, "and that's precisely what Rabbi Abraham Geiger called them—'too extreme.' But perhaps the following incident shows the extent of their radicalism even better. As a result of improper circumcision," he related, "several Jewish babies of Frankfort had died, and the city's Sanitary Bureau demanded that all future circumcisions be conducted under its supervision. The law that was passed stated: 'Jewish citizens, insofar as they desire to have their children circumcised, must employ only persons officially appointed to perform this rite.'

"Immediately, some members of the Reform Society interpreted this to mean that it was no longer necessary to have their children circumcised, and several refused to have the rite performed. The Orthodox rabbi of Frankfort urged the Senate to clarify the law so that Jews should not think that circumcision was optional, but the Senate refused. The rabbi appealed to other rabbis of Europe for support of his position, and forty-one replies were received from Orthodox and Reform rabbis unanimously condemning the action of the Reform Society members."

"The radicals seem to have preferred doing away with Jewish practices," Mother ventured the opinion, "instead of trying to adjust them to modern conditions."

"That's right, and that was the principal objection of the more moderate Reformers," agreed Great-Grandfather. "However, the immediate result was a controversy within Reform ranks which threatened to split the young movement."

Problem Two: The Need for Common Reform Practice. "What other problems were there?" Father asked.

"There was an urgent need for common Reform practice," Great-Grandfather answered. "In the early days there were vast differences in practice between the various Reform temples springing up all over Europe. In some congregations minor reforms, such as the use of the language of the country for prayers and sermons, were adopted. In others, as in the case of the Berlin Reform Society, more extensive changes were introduced. By 1845, for example, its worship was conducted almost wholly in German. It held special services on Sunday morning, permitted women to participate in worship equally with men, and eliminated the wearing of hats and talesim."

"But why was this a problem?" Mother wanted to know.

"Because," Great-Grandfather pointed out, "people were so confused by the differences between temples and the various claims of radical and moderate Reformers that they wondered which represented Reform Judaism. As early as January 15, 1844, Ludwig Philippson, the editor of the widely-read German weekly, the *Jewish News,* realized the problem and publicly appealed for a rabbinical conference to decide the question. 'What form our religion should take,' he wrote, 'is the major issue today.'

"As a result, a rabbinical conference was arranged for June 12 through 19 of that year, and twenty-four rabbis gathered in Brunswick 'to consider ways and means for the preservation of Judaism and the awakening of the Jewish spirit.' "

Problem Three: Did Judaism Accept Change? "But," Betty argued, "the Orthodox refused to sanction even minor changes. What right, then, had any group of rabbis to conduct such a conference?"

Great-Grandfather smiled. "You've just stated Reform's third problem," he declared. "Reform leaders agreed

that the modernization of Judaism was a necessity and that unless reforms were promptly introduced, thousands of Jews might abandon their faith. But Orthodox rabbis accepted no distinction between important and minor practices. To them all were sacred and unchangeable. Reform, therefore, had to prove that Judaism could rightfully be changed.

"It was here that the movement received its greatest assistance from Leopold Zunz, one of the outstanding German-Jewish scholars of the nineteenth century. Zunz had served as preacher at the Berlin Reform services held in the home of Jacob Herz Beer, and when, in 1823, the government ordered them discontinued, he undertook a scientific study of Jewish history and literature to determine whether in the past Judaism had permitted change. In 1832,

Leopold Zunz

replying to the government's charge that preaching in German was a radically new idea in Judaism, Zunz published his famous book, *The Historical Development of the Jewish Sermon*. In it he proved that it was an old practice of Judaism to have sermons preached in any language that Jews could understand, and that the Talmud sanctioned even prayers in languages other than Hebrew. Zunz also showed that throughout the years new prayers had been constantly added to the Jewish ritual."

"So Judaism could change!" Betty said enthusiastically.

"Unquestionably. Zunz's scientific study of Jewish history conclusively proved that in the past Judaism had always adjusted itself to the needs of the people, and he argued that those who objected to reforms did so from ignorance and prejudice, not from a real knowledge of Judaism. As time progressed, other Jewish scholars uncovered further historical evidence to support Reform's view of a Judaism that changed with the times."

Problem Four: What Changes Were Needed? (1) *Synagogue Worship.* Father asked the next question. "What were some of the actual reforms that were being suggested?"

"I'm sure that people were asking for changes in synagogue worship," Betty called out.

"Yes, the Reformers were certainly interested in that," agreed Great-Grandfather. "Many Jews no longer understood the all-Hebrew ritual of the Orthodox synagogue. They were distracted by the constant hubbub of the congregation and the hasty chanting of the service. In fact, the rendition of the Torah portion had become so unintelligible that many congregants spent the time conversing with one another, or else left the synagogue. Reformers, therefore, insisted upon an orderly service with the reading of some prayers in German, a weekly sermon, and the translation of the Torah reading. . . ."

"And the use of the organ," Betty reminded him.

"They not only advocated the use of the organ which had been banned from the Orthodox synagogue," Great-Grandfather agreed, "but they also called for the singing by a mixed choir of men and women and the translation of certain congregational hymns into German."

"I think the temple music is the most inspiring part of the service," Mother commented. "This was certainly an important contribution to Jewish worship."

"The Reform prayer book is another," Father chimed in. "To me the English prayers are as impressive as the Hebrew." And then turning to Great-Grandfather, he said, "But please go on. What were other Reform proposals?"

(2) *Belief in the Messiah.* "Reform leaders," Great-Grandfather replied,

"wanted a revision of the Orthodox beliefs concerning the Messiah."

"What do you mean by that?" questioned Mother.

Great-Grandfather hastened to explain. "Ever since the Jewish State was destroyed and the people were forced to leave Palestine, Orthodox Judaism maintained that the Jew was in exile. Naturally, the unhappy experiences of Jews in the countries of Europe reinforced this belief.

"Therefore, our people prayed for someone to deliver them—for the coming of the Messiah, a powerful descendant of King David, to lead them back to Palestine. There they would rebuild the Temple and restore the ancient sacrifices. The dead, too, would return to life and rejoin their people. These hopes were, of course, expressed in many prayers recited in the synagogue."

"And what was the attitude of the Reformers?" asked Father.

It was Betty who answered. "I know the reason. They were opposed to such prayers. Now that Jews had been granted citizenship they no longer had cause to consider themselves exiles."

"There was still another objection, Betty," Great-Grandfather added. "Many thinking Jews found it hard to believe that the appearance of any single individual—even a Messiah—could change the entire world or restore the dead to life. A Messianic Age, they felt, would arrive only when every person became

wholly righteous. Then, and only then, would our world find lasting peace and happiness."

(3) *The Religious Rights of Women.* Mother spoke up. "I would say that improving the religious position of Jewish women was another badly-needed reform. Even today wives are not allowed to sit with their husbands at Orthodox services. . . ."

"Reform leaders, of course, were advocating religious equality for Jewish women," Great-Grandfather stated, "because, except for the opportunity to pray with the congregation, our women enjoyed few other religious rights. They were compelled to sit in the less desirable women's section, and because they were prohibited from sitting with men it was impossible for the synagogue to have the singing of a mixed choir. Women were not included in a minyon, the quorum of ten Jews required for worship; nor could they serve as witnesses in matters involving Jewish ritual.

"The Reformers argued that the inferior position of women had originated in the Orient where the Jews had formerly lived. But now that they were part of the Western world where women participated more fully in religious life, Judaism, in keeping with its belief in democracy, should extend them complete equality."

"That's something for which Reform can well take credit," Mother said emphatically.

Great-Grandfather heartily agreed.

(4) *Sabbath and Holiday Observance.* It was Betty's turn to raise a question. "Weren't there also some problems connected with observing the Sabbath?" she asked. "Mildred told me that Orthodox Judaism forbids riding on Shabos. Now if that's true, how could some people get to services?"

"This was one of the difficulties," Great-Grandfather responded. "After Jews moved out of the ghetto, some, as Betty has mentioned, lived too far to walk to synagogue services. But," he continued, "modern conditions created other hardships for those who wanted to observe the Sabbath. Many Jews, for instance, were now compelled to earn their livelihood by working on the Sabbath. Yet the definition of Sabbath 'rest' prohibited attending to business, riding, recreation, and lots of other activities."

"What answers did Reform have?" asked Mother.

"A few of the rabbis advocated holding an additional service on Sunday so that all Jews could attend worship. Many others proposed that Judaism permit riding to the synagogue and other essential activities on the Sabbath."

"And what was the problem about Jewish holiday observance?" Father reminded Great-Grandfather.

"The principal question there involved the extra days of the Jewish holidays," answered Great-Grandfather. "When Jews began living outside of Palestine, the rabbis added an extra day of observance to the holidays lest, through accident or the failure of word to travel from Jerusalem to outlying communities, they be celebrated on the wrong dates. Thus, instead of commemorating Shovuos for one day as commanded in the Bible, all Jews outside of Palestine were required to observe two days."

"Reform did away with the extra days, didn't it?" Mother questioned.

"Yes," Great-Grandfather asserted, "now that the Jewish calendar could be scientifically calculated for hundreds of years in advance, and there was no longer any danger of observing the wrong day, Reform leaders saw no reason for keeping the extra days. They proposed that the Jewish holidays be celebrated according to the original number of days mentioned in the Bible."

"That seems reasonable," Father commented.

"I notice," Mother remarked, "that Reform Judaism also created new ceremonies for some of the holidays —like Confirmation on Shovuos."

"That was part of modernizing the Jewish holidays," declared Great-Grandfather. "Reform believes in reinterpreting the holidays and making them more meaningful for modern Jews."

(5) *Jewish Marriage and Divorce Laws.* "But," Great-Grandfather went on, "there were two other areas in which reforms were badly needed. One involved the Jewish marriage and divorce laws, since in ghetto days the whole of Jewish life had been regulated by Jewish law, and this included special requirements for marriage and divorce. But now as new citizens, Jews were subject to the civil law of the countries in which they lived. Nevertheless, in matters of marriage and divorce, Orthodox rabbis insisted that the people continue to abide by all of the Jewish as well as civil laws."

"Suppose a Jew was granted a civil divorce but did not receive his Jewish divorce," Father cited as an example, "could he remarry according to Orthodox Judaism?"

"No," stated Great-Grandfather, "and this made for considerable difficulty and confusion. Furthermore, there were some Orthodox regulations that worked serious hardships on women."

"For instance?" Mother asked.

"The case of the 'Aguno,' the woman whose husband had disappeared. Because there had been no actual witnesses to his death, she could never remarry."

"How terrible!" Mother cried.

"Such cases," Great-Grandfather stated, "prompted Reform leaders to urge that Judaism retain only the most essential marriage and divorce regulations. With the exception of these, Judaism should then accept the decisions of civil law."

(6) *Jewish Mourning Customs.* "Jewish mourning customs," Great-Grandfather went on, "was the other area in which changes were suggested. . . ."

Father broke in. "You know," he remarked, "I was just thinking about that. I recall a visit that I made recently to an Orthodox couple who had lost their father. Some of their mourning practices really surprised me. They were required to make a small cut in one of their garments and sit on low stools or on the ground. . . ."

"They weren't permitted to wash or shave or wear their shoes," Mother declared.

"And, of course," Father added, "they had to stay at home throughout the seven-day mourning period."

"The Reformers also questioned such practices," Great-Grandfather commented, "and they noted the financial hardship a seven-day mourning period often caused many families. Yes," he agreed, "some revision of Jewish mourning customs was definitely indicated."

The Family Makes a Prediction. "In other words," Betty summed up, "Reform had to meet four problems. First, it had to protect Judaism against the extremes of the Reform radicals; second, provide the movement with common practices; third,

WHY REFORM SOUGHT CHANGES IN JEWISH PRACTICES

	The Situation in Orthodoxy	Why Reform Desired Changes
SYNAGOGUE WORSHIP	All-Hebrew ritual Long, repetitious service with all prayers chanted Organ and mixed choir barred Lack of order during worship	All-Hebrew service difficult to understand Service lengthy because of many repetitions Chanting made worship unintelligible Reformers sought inspiring synagogue music and a quiet, worshipful atmosphere
BELIEF IN THE MESSIAH	Prayed for the coming of a personal Messiah to deliver the Jews from "exile" and restore them to Palestine Prayed for the rebuilding of the Temple and restoration of sacrifices Dead to be restored to life and returned to Palestine	As citizens Jews no longer considered themselves in "exile" or desired to return to Palestine Judaism had outgrown the ancient practice of sacrifices and burnt-offerings and the belief that the dead could be restored to life Modern Jews felt that the Messianic Age would come when all men became righteous
THE RELIGIOUS RIGHTS OF WOMEN	Women compelled to sit by themselves in a special synagogue section Women barred from participating actively in the service Women not counted toward a minyon or permitted to serve as witnesses in ritual matters	Reform maintained that the position of women in Orthodoxy had originated in the East. Now that most Jews lived in the West, Judaism should adopt the western standards of greater religious equality for women
SABBATH AND HOLIDAY OBSERVANCE	No riding to the synagogue permitted on the Sabbath Sabbath "rest" prohibited many types of activities, including essential work Extra days were added to each of the major Jewish holidays	Many Jews lived too far from synagogue to walk on Sabbath Modern conditions required many Jews to work on the Sabbath which also prevented them attending worship Since the calendar could now be calculated exactly, it was felt that there was no further reason for continuing the extra days of the holidays
JEWISH MARRIAGE AND DIVORCE LAWS	Many Jewish laws regulating marriage and divorce Jewish laws worked a special hardship on women	Now that Jews were citizens and subject to civil law, the many Jewish laws made for confusion Those Jewish laws which worked a special hardship on women were out of keeping with the times
JEWISH MOURNING CUSTOMS	Mourners required to make a small cut in one of their garments, sit on the ground, and refrain from shaving, bathing and wearing shoes Mourners expected to observe a 7-day mourning period	Orthodox mourning customs were looked upon as meaningless in modern times Frequently a 7-day mourning period caused financial hardship to the family

establish the fact that Judaism permitted change; and fourth, determine the actual practices which Reform Jews were to observe."

Father spoke up. "Don't you mean three problems, Betty? Didn't Reform leaders already prove that Judaism welcomed change?"

"That's right," Great-Grandfather admitted. "That leaves just three. . . ."

"It seems to me," Mother broke in, "that there was really only one problem. It was simply a matter of determining Reform's beliefs and practices. Then the difficulties with the radical Reformers and the differences between the various Reform congregations would automatically be settled."

"A good point," Great-Grandfather acknowledged. "So, you see, actually it all boiled down to one question—what were to be the beliefs and practices of the Reform Jew?"

"Well," Betty prodded him, "what was done about it?"

Great-Grandfather had a twinkle in his eye. "Let's see how good this family is at predicting," he said. "How do you think Reform settled the matter?"

Mother went first. "That seems fairly simple," she said. "Everybody knew what changes were needed, so they called a meeting of representative Reform members. . . ."

"No, no," Father interrupted, "not Reform members, Reform *rabbis*. They met at . . . er . . . what was the name of that place?"

Betty supplied the missing name. "Brunswick," she called out. "You told us they met there for a week, Great-Grandfather. They must have settled the whole thing then, eh?"

Great-Grandfather wore a broad smile. "You were all almost right," he grinned. "You missed it by only . . . twenty-seven years!"

"Twenty-seven years!" the family gasped.

"What on earth took them so long?" Father demanded.

"Meetings," answered Great-Grandfather simply.

"They must have been mighty important meetings to last that long," Mother commented dryly.

"They were," replied Great-Grandfather. "Let me tell you about them. . . ."

QUESTIONS FOR DISCUSSION

1. Why were the Reform radicals a problem to the young movement?
2. Why was the development of common Reform practices necessary?
3. How does Reform justify its right to make changes in Judaism?
4. Why did the Reformers demand changes in Orthodox synagogue practices, Sabbath and holiday observances, and mourning customs?
5. Why did the Reformers object to the traditional beliefs concerning the Messiah?
6. In what ways are the attitudes of the Reformers toward the religious rights of Jewish women reflected in the practices of your temple today?

1. Invite a person well informed on Orthodox Judaism to discuss the various practices which were problems to the early Reform movement.
2. Attend an Orthodox wedding or some other Orthodox ceremony and compare it with the corresponding Reform practice.
3. Prepare a series of slides or posters which show the differences between the important Reform and Orthodox practices as carried on in your community.

GOLUB, JACOB S. and ALAN S. GREEN, *A Short History of the Jews, III,* pp. 16-17.

SOLOFF, MORDECAI I., *How the Jewish People Lives Today,* pp. 138-149.

References for the Teacher

FREEHOF, SOLOMON B., *Reform Jewish Practice,* "Public Worship," pp. 16-55; "Marriage and Divorce," pp. 56-110; "Burial and Mourning," pp. 115-183.

Jewish Encyclopedia, "Agunah," Vol. 1, pp. 275-276; "Divorce," Vol. 4, pp. 624-628; "Marriage," Vol. 8, pp. 347-349; "Mourning," Vol. 9, pp. 101-103; "Sabbath," Vol. 10, pp. 591-602; "Leopold Zunz," Vol. 12, pp. 699-704.

PHILIPSON, DAVID, *The Reform Movement in Judaism,* Chap. 6, "The Frankfort Society of the Friends of Reform."

SCHWARTZMAN, SYLVAN D., *Reform Judaism in the Making,* Chap. 7, "The Need for Reform Direction."

Universal Jewish Encyclopedia, "Agunah," Vol. 1, pp. 132-133; "Divorce," Vol. 3, pp. 577-580; "Covering of Head," Vol. 5, pp. 262-263; "Marriage," Vol. 7, pp. 370-376; "Messiah," Vol. 7, pp. 499-503; "Mourning," Vol. 8, pp. 28-31; "Musical Instruments," Vol. 8, pp. 55-56.

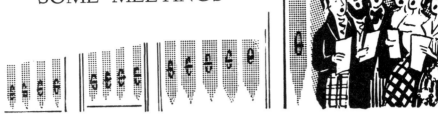

8. REFORM HOLDS SOME MEETINGS

Great-Grandfather Produces His Clippings. "Yes," Great-Grandfather repeated, "from 1844 to 1871 the Reformers tried to settle many of the problems of Jewish belief and practice. . . ."

"Imagine!" exclaimed Mother, "twenty-seven years of meetings!"

"Actually they held only five meetings in all that time," explained Great-Grandfather.

The Brunswick Synagogue in Germany. It was in the city of Brunswick that early reforms of Judaism were discussed.

"Why so few?" Betty asked.

"And what did they finally decide?" Father wanted to know.

Great-Grandfather threw up his hands. "If you'll just wait a minute," he suggested, "you'll have the answers to all your questions." He reached up on the mantel and Betty recognized the large scrap-book of clippings.

"The whole story's right here," he announced to the family as he opened the volume and thumbed through it until he found what he was looking for. "There," he said with satisfaction. "Now suppose you all gather round and read while I hunt up a chart of the achievements of the Reform conferences I once made." With that he left the room.

Father picked up the scrap-book and Mother and Betty looked on. There, pasted across the page was one of a series of old, yellowed newspaper clippings. The first one told about the call for the Brunswick Rabbinical Conference—

CALL FOR CONFERENCE HEEDED; RABBIS TO MEET IN BRUNSWICK

Editor's Plea for Rabbinical Conference Produces Results; Meeting in June to Consider Needed Revisions of Judaism

BRUNSWICK, April 15, 1844—It was announced today that the appeal of Ludwig Philippson, editor of the well-known German weekly, the *Jewish News*, for a rabbinical conference to consider revisions of Jewish belief and practice according to the needs of the day, has met with success. The gathering has been set for June 12-19 in this city, and it is expected that there will be a good attendance of Liberal rabbis.

The question of reforms in Judaism has been one that has concerned the Jews of Europe ever since their emancipation. As early as August, 1837, Rabbi Abraham Geiger held a rabbinical conference at Wiesbaden to grapple with the same issue, but the gathering accomplished practically nothing.

A resolution was passed that should be published at Brunswick

The account broke off suddenly where the bottom portion of the clipping was torn away.

MAP OF REFORM DEVELOPMENTS IN EUROPE

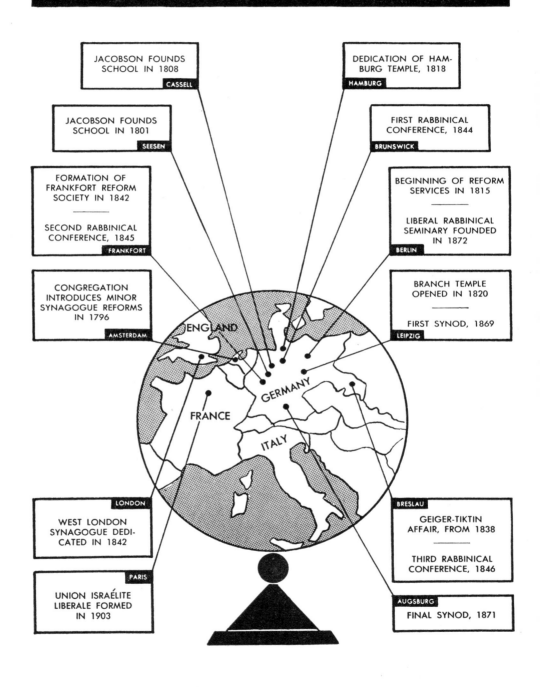

JACOBSON FOUNDS
SCHOOL IN 1808
CASSELL

JACOBSON FOUNDS
SCHOOL IN 1801
SEESEN

FORMATION OF
FRANKFORT REFORM
SOCIETY IN 1842

SECOND RABBINICAL
CONFERENCE, 1845
FRANKFORT

CONGREGATION
INTRODUCES MINOR
SYNAGOGUE REFORMS
IN 1796
AMSTERDAM

DEDICATION OF HAM-
BURG TEMPLE, 1818
HAMBURG

FIRST RABBINICAL
CONFERENCE, 1844
BRUNSWICK

BEGINNING OF REFORM
SERVICES IN 1815
―――――
LIBERAL RABBINICAL
SEMINARY FOUNDED
IN 1872
BERLIN

BRANCH TEMPLE
OPENED IN 1820
―――――
FIRST SYNOD, 1869
LEIPZIG

ENGLAND

FRANCE

GERMANY

ITALY

LONDON
WEST LONDON
SYNAGOGUE DEDI-
CATED IN 1842

PARIS
UNION ISRAÉLITE
LIBERALE FORMED
IN 1903

BRESLAU
GEIGER-TIKTIN
AFFAIR, FROM 1838
―――――
THIRD RABBINICAL
CONFERENCE, 1846

AUGSBURG
FINAL SYNOD, 1871

The Conference at Brunswick. Father turned the page and this was the next newspaper clipping that appeared:

RABBIS REACH NO AGREEMENT; COMMITTEES TO STUDY ISSUES

Delegates Defend Right to Make Changes in Jewish Law; 7 Questions to Be Investigated for Next Year's Meeting

BRUNSWICK, June 19, 1844—Twenty-four Liberal European rabbis, among them Abraham Geiger, met here from June 12 until today but failed to arrive at a common agreement on Reform practices. While many of the delegates insisted that the Conference had the right to make changes in basic Jewish law, the rabbis did not adopt any official resolution on this important subject. Instead, they merely appointed special committees to study and report on seven of the most pressing issues.

The questions under investigation, of which four involve synagogue practices, include: (1) the amount of Hebrew to be retained in worship; (2) abbreviation of the length of the service, especially through elimination of repetitious prayers; (3) use of the organ in worship; (4) improvement of certain synagogue practices, such as the manner of reading the Torah; (5) changes in Jewish marriage regulations; (6) modifications of Sabbath restrictions; and (7) revision of traditional beliefs about the Messiah.

Before adjourning, the rabbis voted to meet next year in Frankfort where the various committees will present their recommendations.

There has been a variety of reactions to the Brunswick Conference. As was expected, Orthodox spokesmen have denounced it as "destructive" and "slanderous toward Judaism." Ludwig Philippson, who was present at the sessions, expressed some disappointment with the failure of the delegates to take definite action on the issues before them. In general, however, most Reform quarters are not discouraged by the results. They feel that the Conference, wisely, moved slowly in order to lay proper foundations for future accomplishments.

Frankfort, 1845—The Second Rabbinical Conference. The clipping on the next page dealt with the Frankfort Conference held a year later.

CONFERENCE APPROVES REFORMS; INTRODUCES CHANGES IN WORSHIP

Shortened Liturgy, Use of Organ in Worship Sanctioned; Committees to Study Mourning Customs, Women's Rights

FRANKFORT, July 28, 1845—A two-week meeting in this city of thirty Liberal rabbis adjourned today after reaching a number of important decisions in the area of synagogue reforms.

The Conference which began July 15 agreed that major prayers, such as the "Sh'ma," as well as the reading of the Torah, should be retained in Hebrew, and that the service should be shortened by the elimination of all repetition in the ritual.

The delegates also approved the use of the organ in worship, and they replaced the idea of the coming of a personal Messiah to deliver the Jews out of "exile" with the belief in a Messianic Age of peace and justice for all mankind.

Previously-appointed committees on Sabbath observance and Jewish marriage regulations, as well as new committees on mourning customs and the religious rights of women, were asked to report their findings at the Conference scheduled for next year at Breslau.

The Last Rabbinical Conference—Breslau, 1846. The next item was a newspaper account of the final rabbinical conference, and it read:

RABBIS ADOPT SABBATH REFORMS; ALSO HOLIDAY, MOURNING CHANGES

Time Is Lacking to Decide on Women's Religious Rights; Leaders Propose Future Conferences Also Include Laymen

BRESLAU, July 24, 1846—During their eleven-day meeting the twenty-three delegates to a rabbinical conference held in this city adopted sweeping changes in religious practices involving the Sabbath, holidays, and mourning customs.

Work on the Sabbath was declared permissible wherever necessary for one's livelihood and by those engaged in public service. However, the delegates rejected a proposal to overcome most problems of Sabbath observance by transferring the Jewish Sabbath to Sunday.

The Conference eliminated the extra days of all Jewish holidays except Rosh Ha-shono, which is observed for two days even in Palestine.

The mourning period was shortened to three days with the closing of business on the day of burial, and regulations about washing, shaving, bathing, cutting a portion of one's clothes, and the seating of the family have been abolished.

Because of lack of time a committee report recommending equal religious rights for women could not be acted upon.

The executive committee of the Conference has proposed that future decisions be made by a synod, a joint meeting of rabbis and laymen.

How the Rabbis Reached Their Decisions. Father put down the scrapbook and turned to Great-Grandfather who was just coming into the room. "What was the Jewish reaction to these rabbinical conferences?" he asked.

"In general," he responded, "Reform leaders were satisfied with the progress that was being made. Of course, there were many religious issues that still remained, but it was hoped that future meetings would settle them.

"Two groups, however, were very critical of the results," he disclosed. "One, of course, was the Orthodox. They were greatly disturbed by the changes that had been made and they accused the Reformers of destroying the Jewish religion. The other group was the radical Reformers who condemned the rabbis for not having gone far enough in the changes they advocated. Thus, for instance, they criticized the Breslau Rabbinical Conference for having failed to transfer the Jewish Sabbath to Sunday."

"Why didn't they adopt this change?" Mother asked him.

"Because the rabbis were guided in their decisions by their careful investigation of traditional Jewish teachings. Actually, these conferences did not change our religion; they merely utilized already-existing Jewish principles to modernize it. For instance, in permitting the use of German in worship, the rabbis based their decision upon the Talmud which stated that even the Sh'ma could be recited in any language which Jews understood. And where the rabbis believed that Jewish tradition justified the preservation of old practices—as in the case of maintaining the Sabbath on Saturday—they so decided. Naturally, the thorough study and discussion of each question was a slow process, but the rabbis preferred to base their reforms on a complete understanding of the teachings of Judaism. Hence, it was necessary to hold a number of conferences before various reforms could be adopted."

The Leipzig Synod, 1869. Seeing that there were no further questions, the family turned once more to the scrapbook. The next clipping dealt with the Leipzig Synod of 1869.

LITTLE ACCOMPLISHED BY LEIPZIG SYNOD; FAVORS ONLY PREVIOUSLY-ADOPTED REFORMS

83 Delegates Representing 11 Countries Attend Meeting; Fail to Adopt New Decisions on Jewish Practices, Beliefs

LEIPZIG, July 4, 1869—The first Reform gathering in 23 years, during which Jews were too occupied with Europe's political struggles to preserve freedom to meet on questions of religious change, adjourned today after a full week of deliberations.

The Synod, comprising 49 laymen and 34 rabbis representing 60 congregations of Germany, Austria, Belgium, Bohemia, Hungary, England, Galicia, Rumania, Switzerland, the United States, and the West Indies, did little more, however, than reaffirm the decisions of previous rabbinical conferences. It gave its approval to the use of languages other than Hebrew in the service and the playing of the organ during worship.

In addition, the delegates voted to permit a mixed choir in the synagogue and urged the creation of an inspiring memorial service for Yom Kippur.

Many Reform leaders appear keenly disappointed with the results. "The delegates spent most of the time talking about minor changes," one spokesman declared.

The Last Synod—Augsburg, 1871. On the very last page of the scrap-book appeared this clipping about the final European Reform synod:

SYNOD REVISES MARRIAGE LAWS; GRANTS WOMEN GREATER RIGHTS

Delegates Give Approval to Essential Riding on Sabbath; Committee Named to Study Reforms of Jewish Divorce Laws

AUGSBURG, July 17, 1871—Postponed for a year because of the outbreak of the Franco-Prussian War, the Synod meeting in this city reached important decisions in the course of its week-long discussions which closed today.

The 52 delegates from 30 congregations of Germany, Austria, Hungary, Galicia, and Switzerland adopted reforms of the Jewish marriage laws. These include permission to hold a double-ring ceremony, the elimination of most days on which weddings have been forbidden, and acceptance of a legal certificate of death issued by the civil courts in the case of the missing husband of an "Aguno," thus enabling her to remarry.

Riding on the Sabbath, whenever necessary for religious, charitable, or educational purposes, was sanctioned. Greater rights for women, too, were approved. They were given a more active part in the wedding ceremony and were declared proper witnesses in Jewish ritual matters.

Another action of the Synod was the recommendation that Chanuko, which until now has been regarded as a minor holiday, be observed with greater celebration; and a committee was also appointed by the Augsburg Synod to study and propose reforms of the Jewish divorce laws.

While Reform leaders are highly pleased with the accomplishments, the Synod's decision to modify marriage regulations has called forth a storm of protest from 133 Orthodox rabbis who have stated that marriages performed on this basis will not be regarded as Jewish. They have also demanded that all Reform rabbis be discharged from their positions; and where this is not possible, Orthodox members have been asked to resign and form new congregations.

What the Conferences and Synods Achieved. When the family finished the account of the Augsburg Synod, Great-Grandfather brought forward a large chart. "Here," he said, holding it aloft, "is a bird's-eye view of

ACCOMPLISHMENTS OF THE EUROPEAN CONFERENCES AND SYNODS

Problem	Brunswick Conference	Frankfort Conference	Breslau Conference	Leipzig Synod	Augsburg Synod
RELIGIOUS SERVICES	Committee appointed to study various improvements in worship, the repetition of prayers, and the use of the organ and Hebrew	Approved the use of the language of the land and of the organ Some Hebrew to be retained Repetitious prayers eliminated		Use of the organ and mixed choir approved Haftoro portion to be read in translation	
MESSIANIC BELIEFS	Committee appointed to study the question	Removed prayers for the coming of a personal Messiah and deliverance from exile Substituted a belief in the coming of a Messianic Age		Substituted belief in the coming of a Messianic Age in place of a personal Messiah	
RELIGIOUS RIGHTS OF WOMEN		Committee appointed to study the question	Committee recommended equal rights for women	Committee appointed to study the question	Women declared eligible to serve as witnesses in ritual matters
SABBATH OBSERVANCE	Committee appointed to study the question		Riding to the synagogue permitted Essential work on the Sabbath approved		Riding on the Sabbath for religious, charitable and educational purposes approved
HOLIDAY OBSERVANCE		Committee appointed to study the question	All extra days of the holidays except Rosh Hashono eliminated	Suggested creation of inspiring memorial service on Yom Kippur	Wider celebration of Chanuko proposed
MARRIAGE REGULATIONS	Committee appointed to study the question			Committee appointed to study the question	Bride to participate actively in ceremony Double-ring ceremony permitted Most days forbidden for marriage abolished "Aguno" remarriage permitted
DIVORCE LAWS				Committee on marriage regulations to study the question	Committee appointed to study the question
MOURNING CUSTOMS		Committee appointed to study the question	Orthodox mourning practices ended 3-day period set		

what the various conferences and synods accomplished in trying to decide upon Reform practices and beliefs."

The family examined the chart closely.

"Quite a number of distinctive Reform contributions came out of these meetings," Mother asserted as she looked over the chart. "There's the revival of Chanuko as an important Jewish holiday, the new emphasis on synagogue music, and the translation of many portions of the service," she listed.

"And the conferences and synods seem to have solved many of the Reform problems we discussed," Father added.

"Perhaps as important as the accomplishments which appear on the chart," Great-Grandfather said, "is the fact that Reform leaders insisted upon making their changes on the basis of Jewish tradition itself. In this way, Reform represented a developing Judaism and not a separate sect."

Why Didn't European Reform Progress? "I notice," observed Betty as she continued to examine the chart, "that the conferences and synods never did settle certain problems, such as revisions of the Jewish divorce laws. They only appointed a committee to study the question at the last synod." She paused a moment. "I bet there were still other reforms that were needed."

"Right you are, Betty," Great-Grandfather admitted, "and they never were achieved in Europe. We have to go to America for that."

"Why?" asked Mother. "What happened to Reform in Europe?"

"I've been wondering about that, too, ever since I discovered that Reform originated in Europe and not in the United States," remarked Father.

"Well," Great-Grandfather replied, "you can be sure that European Reform didn't disappear. But it certainly failed to make much more progress. . . ."

"That seems very peculiar," Mother commented, "especially since the movement got its start in Europe."

"There's probably a good reason for it," said Father.

"There certainly is," Great-Grandfather declared. "In fact, there are at least *six* good reasons. . . ."

QUESTIONS FOR DISCUSSION

1. Why did it take so long for European Reform to reach decisions on various Jewish practices and beliefs?

2. Why did the conferences and synods insist upon the support of Jewish tradition in the changes they made?

3. What were the decisions reached by European Reform on the questions of religious services, Sabbath and holiday observances, and mourning customs?

4. What changes did European Reform make in traditional Messianic beliefs and marriage regulations?

5. In what areas of religious practice and belief did European Reform fail to reach decisions?

6. How do the decisions of the European conferences and synods compare with the practices of your Reform temple today?

SUGGESTED ACTIVITIES

1. Prepare a magazine article describing the accomplishments and shortcomings of the European Reform rabbinical conferences and synods.

2. Let the class serve as a European Reform synod in discussing and reaching decisions on the various problems considered by European Reform.

3. Prepare a chart comparing the decisions reached by European Reform with the present practices carried on in your temple.

ADDITIONAL READINGS FOR PUPILS

SOLOFF, MORDECAI I., *How the Jewish People Lives Today*, pp. 146-149.

References for the Teacher

Central Conference of American Rabbis Yearbook, Vol. 1, pp. 85-117 (the results of the various European conferences and synods).

Jewish Encyclopedia, "Rabbinical Conferences," Vol. 4, pp. 211-214; "Ludwig Philippson," Vol. 9, p. 684.

PHILIPSON, DAVID, *The Reform Movement in Judaism,* Chap. 7, "The Rabbinical Conferences, 1844-46"; Chap. 11, "The Leipzig and Augsburg Synods."

SCHWARTZMAN, SYLVAN D., *Reform Judaism in the Making,* Chap. 8, "Three Decades of Conferences, 1844–1871."

Universal Jewish Encyclopedia, "Rabbinical Conferences," Vol. 3, pp. 327-328; "Ludwig Philippson," Vol. 8, p. 487.

9. WHY REFORM FAILED IN EUROPE

A Puzzling Situation. It was really puzzling to the Friedberg family. Here Reform Judaism had originated in Europe; Reform societies and congregations were springing up all over the Continent, and the rabbinical conferences and synods were successfully modernizing many Jewish beliefs and practices. All in all, the movement seemed to be progressing.

Then, according to Great-Grandfather, Reform ceased to make any real advances in Europe, and the story of its development now shifted to the United States.

Father, Mother, and Betty all wondered about it. Yes, this certainly was something that needed explaining.

Betty fidgeted. "Well, Great-Grandfather, we're waiting. . . ."

"Yes," Mother and Father chimed in, "what prevented Reform's growth in Europe?"

Great-Grandfather finally spoke. "All right," he agreed, "I'll explain. As I mentioned before, there were at least six good reasons for the failure of European Reform. . . ."

Reason #1—Setbacks in Freedom. "The political insecurity of the European Jew," Great-Grandfather announced, "was the first and perhaps main reason. . . ."

Betty protested. "But, you told us that the French Revolution freed the Jews of Germany, France, Italy, and many other countries. . . ."

"Originally, that was true," he answered, "but we mustn't forget that the new freedoms suffered a setback in 1815 when Napoleon was defeated at the Battle of Waterloo. With his surrender, most of the ex-kings of Europe were restored to their thrones. They naturally feared the democratic ideas which the French had introduced and tried in every way to stifle them.

"The first victims were usually the Jews. While many Europeans fought against the loss of their own liberties, few of them were concerned with the fate of their Jewish fellow citizens. Thus, almost as soon as the French armies had withdrawn from Frankfort, Jews were compelled to return to the ghetto. Lübeck and Bremen, two other German cities, expelled most of their Jewish residents—and so on, throughout Europe.

"Furthermore, the kings found Jewish persecution useful. By blaming the Jews for many of the troubles that followed the war with the French, they cleverly shifted responsibility and criticism from themselves. In Germany, while the authorities closed their eyes to the situation, mobs attacked and robbed the Jews of Würzburg, Hamburg, Carlsruhe, Heidelberg, Mannheim, and Frankfort. 'Death to the Jews!' was the cry that rang out all over Germany, and some of the best-known Germans, like the author Goethe, openly expressed hatred of the Jews.

"The Jews of Austria, too, found old discriminations restored. Restrictions in occupations, such as farming, were reintroduced. No additional Jews were permitted to take up residence in Vienna, and those already living there were compelled to pay a special 'toleration tax' and endure other disabilities.

"In Italy the Jewish situation was much worse. When Napoleon's armies left the country, the Pope forced the Jews of Rome to surrender their new homes and return to the miserable ghetto along the Tiber River.

Jews were allowed to trade only within the ghetto; and, once again, they were forced to listen to special sermons designed to convert them to Christianity.

"Even in France, Jews serving as witnesses were humiliated with special Jewish oaths. Before testifying in court, they were compelled to go to the synagogue and, in the presence of the judge, the rabbi, and ten Jewish witnesses, swear that their testimony would be truthful. Furthermore, the Jews of France were obligated to pay toward the maintenance of the Christian religion even while they bore the full cost of supporting their own Jewish institutions."

"How did all this affect the Reform movement?" Mother wanted to know.

"Naturally it hurt its growth," replied Great-Grandfather. "After all, Reform was seeking to adjust Judaism to modern conditions of emancipation. Where, however, freedom for the Jew was denied, there seemed no need for religious reforms. Thus, every new discrimination against the Jews hindered Reform's advancement. On the other hand, Orthodox Judaism, which had developed under ghetto circumstances, could easily adapt itself to the new conditions. With each setback the Orthodox group was quick to say, 'I told you so.' They insisted that Jews weren't really wanted as citizens and that the movement to modernize Judaism was designed to destroy the religion."

"How did the Reform leaders answer that argument?" Father asked.

"They insisted that the Jews' loss of liberty was only temporary," Great-Grandfather said. "Their movement, they argued, had to continue with its program of reforms for that day when our people would again be welcomed as full citizens. Remember," he pointed out, "much of the progress that we have already seen—the establishment of Reform societies and new congregations, the conducting of rabbinical conferences and synods—occurred during this very period of reaction."

"And did the Jews ever regain their freedom?" questioned Betty.

"Yes," Great-Grandfather answered, "but only after a long and difficult struggle during which many Jews joined with their fellow countrymen in seeking to overthrow the rule of the kings and revive democracy.

"In France, for instance, success came rather quickly. In 1830 a revolution dethroned the king and restored liberty to the people. As a result French Jews were granted practically complete citizenship, and in 1831 Judaism—along with Protestantism and Catholicism—was declared an official religion entitled to share state support. By 1846, the last legal discrimination—the Jewish oath —was removed.

"In Germany, Austria, and Hungary, a more prolonged struggle took place. In these countries the revolutions of 1848 forced the kings to grant democratic constitutions which, however, they promptly ignored when new reaction set in shortly after. It wasn't until 1867 that the Jews of Austria received equality, and, in Hungary, it was 1896 before Judaism came to be recognized as a legal religion. And, while most Central European Jews were gradually given equal rights on paper, in reality they continued to endure many disabilities.

"They were somewhat more fortunate in northern Italy. As soon as the Austrians were driven from power in 1859, the Italians restored Jewish citizenship. But all the Jews of Italy were not freed until 1871 when the Catholic church was forced to surrender Rome to the Italian people.

"Even in as liberal a country as England, it wasn't until 1858 that the first Jew—Lionel Rothschild— was permitted to become a member of the House of Commons, and it was 1871 before Jews could be awarded degrees at Oxford and Cambridge Universities."

Reason #2—The Rise of Anti-Semitism. "But even where many of our people finally regained most of their rights," Great-Grandfather hastened to point out, "they were constantly fearful of losing them again. . . ."

"Why?" Betty queried.

"Because of the growing wave of prejudice spread by organized anti-

Semitic movements," was his answer.

"In Germany," he went on to illustrate, "anti-Semites circulated the lie that Jews were an 'inferior' people, and a number of important European leaders accepted the idea. As great a scholar as Ernest Renan in 1855 declared this falsehood to be true. More and more the anti-Semites argued that Jews were a 'foreign race who didn't belong in Europe and hence should be driven out.' 'Jews cannot possibly become patriotic citizens of Germany,' a well-known German writer stated in 1872.

"The anti-Semites organized political parties which conducted campaigns of violent Jew-hatred. In Germany, a court-preacher named Adolf Stöcker founded the Christian Socialist Party which campaigned openly against what its leader called 'Jewish domination in business, the press, and politics,' and in 1881 he was elected to the German legislature.

"The following year a convention of German and Austro-Hungarian anti-Semites met in Dresden and urged all European governments to exclude Jews from the army and prevent further Jewish immigration. Many of the old charges against the Jews were revived. Even the lie that they used Christian blood in the celebration of Passover was circulated, and in 1882, in Hungary, fifteen Jews were actually arrested on the charge of ritually murdering a Christian girl who had suddenly disappeared."

"Unbelievable!" exclaimed Mother. "How could modern people believe such fantastic tales?"

"This was only one of many other frightening experiences," Great-Grandfather pointed out, "which contributed to Jewish uneasiness."

"For instance?" Father asked.

"The example of Russia," Great-Grandfather stated. "The democratic influence of the French Revolution had not penetrated Russia, and the country still operated under the old feudal system. Russian Jews still lived as they had under the intolerable conditions of pre-revolutionary Europe. But what was worse, the government deliberately went out of its way to oppress them. Ever fearful of revolt by the Russian people, the government proclaimed the Jews responsible for the wide-spread suffering of the peasants. In this way Russia's tyrant rulers, the Czars, diverted popular attention from their own corrupt regimes.

"In the summer of 1881, mobs organized by the government broke into Jewish sections of hundreds of villages, destroying property, looting, beating and even killing Jews. Now frequent 'pogroms'—attacks on Jews—added to the terror of Russian Jewish life, and they continued until 1917 when the people finally revolted against the Czar. The sad plight of the Russian Jew was always uppermost in the minds of our people.

"But, that wasn't all," Great-

Captain Alfred Dreyfus, right, is about to be reinstated into the French Army. He was completely exonerated and given the rank of Major.

Grandfather went on. "Equally damaging to the morale of the European Jew was the Dreyfus Affair. . . ."

"I've heard about him," Betty spoke up. "Captain Alfred Dreyfus was a Jewish officer on the French Army General Staff who was falsely accused of selling military secrets to the Germans. He was publicly disgraced and sentenced to life-imprisonment, but later was proved totally innocent of any crime."

"That's right, Betty," Great-Grandfather said. "However, the Dreyfus Affair involved much more for the Jews than simply an injustice done to one of them. From Oc-

tober 15, 1894, the day that the captain was first accused, the enemies of democracy used the fact that Dreyfus was a Jew to undermine the French Republic. They condemned the government for permitting 'Jewish traitors' to endanger French safety. They insisted that Jews could not be trusted as citizens, and that any system of government which granted them equality should be abolished. Soon they began to attract a large following of French supporters, and throughout Europe other anti-Semites whipped up popular feeling against democratic rule and Jews. Up until the year 1906, when Dreyfus was finally cleared of all guilt, the Jews of Europe feared that the incident might lead to an end of democratic government and the loss of their liberties."

"I can certainly see how these experiences would harm the Reform movement," observed Father. "If its growth was stunted by the previous political reaction, the spread of anti-Semitism would surely have a similar effect."

"That's true," Great-Grandfather asserted. "Our people constantly felt that they were in danger of losing their liberties, and this sense of Jewish insecurity made it extremely difficult for Reform leaders to convince the masses of our people that Jews were really emancipated and that Judaism should be adjusted to the modern age of freedom."

"And the Orthodox group, of course, took advantage of the situation?" Betty guessed.

"Yes," Great-Grandfather answered, "they hampered the development of Reform in many ways, which brings us to the third reason for its failure in Europe. . . ."

Reason #3—Powerful Orthodox Opposition. "During the growth of the Reform movement," Great-Grandfather explained, "Orthodoxy became even more hostile to change and more determined to keep the Jewish religion as it had been in the ghetto. Wherever possible, the Orthodox took advantage of their over-whelming numbers and position of authority to prevent the adoption of Reform ideas, and in this they were aided by the very nature of European Jewish community organization. Each community was controlled by an elected council which decided all Jewish matters, and no congregation might introduce any reforms unless it had first obtained the council's approval. Being the majority group in most councils, the Orthodox easily stifled Reform attempts at religious change.

"Reform growth was hindered in other ways. In Berlin, for instance, members of the Reform temple not only supported their own congregation but were also compelled by law to pay dues to the main Orthodox synagogue. To cite another example, in 1876, the extreme Orthodox element in Germany led by Samson Raphael Hirsch, the rabbi of Frankfort, had the government pass a law permitting any Jew who disagreed with changes in worship to withdraw from the Jewish community. Because of this, most communities were afraid to introduce reforms. They feared that many of the Orthodox might withdraw and thus deprive the communities of badly needed income."

Mother turned to Great-Grandfather with a question. "Do you mean that the governments actually sided with the Orthodox against the Reform?"

"In many cases, yes," he replied.

"What objection did the govern-

ments have to Reform Judaism?"
Father wanted to know.

"The answer to your question,"
Great-Grandfather stated, "provides
us with the fourth reason for the failure of the movement in Europe. . . ."

**Reason #4—Interference of Reac-
tionary Governments.** "Even if European governments had been favorable
to the cause of Reform," Great-
Grandfather pointed out, "they were
accustomed to recognize the right of
the Jewish community to manage its
own affairs. Since the Orthodox con-
stituted the great majority of the
Jewish community, they were regarded as its spokesman and thereby
received the automatic support of
the government.

"But Orthodox leadership had a
strong ally in the reactionary regimes
of Europe. The restored kings, as we
have already noticed, feared changes
of any sort. They looked upon all
reforms as dangerous to their rule;
and, because Reform Judaism stressed
the idea of religious progress, they
regarded it as a highly undesirable
movement.

"Furthermore, as rulers of over-
whelmingly Christian countries,
many kings considered it part of
their official duty to promote the
growth and influence of the Christian faith. In the growing number of
Jews who were becoming dissatisfied
with Orthodoxy they saw the possi-
bility of many converts to Christianity. Therefore, they tried to hinder

the development of the Reform
movement which sought to meet the
religious needs of these Jews through
the modernization of Judaism.

"In practice, the opposition of the
governments to Reform Judaism
rendered great assistance to the Orthodox. When, for example, the Orthodox appealed to the Prussian king
to halt the Berlin Reform services,
he issued a decree in 1823 that henceforth Jewish services had to be conducted without the slightest innova-
tions in language, ceremonies, prayers, or songs, and Reform activities
in Berlin had to come to an abrupt
end."

**Reason #5—The Rise of the Conserv-
ative Movement.** "Meanwhile,"
Great-Grandfather continued, "the
growth of Reform was also affected
by the appearance of a new movement in Judaism—Conservatism.
Originally, the Conservatives were
part of the Reform group. As the
most moderate wing of the movement, they claimed to support the
idea of progress in Judaism but hesi-
tated to adopt as many or as sweeping changes as the conferences and
synods accepted.

"Interestingly, the Conservative
movement came into existence as the
result of a dispute that occurred during the Brunswick Rabbinical Conference of 1845 over whether the use
of Hebrew in the service was absolutely essential. Zacharias Frankel, a
prominent Liberal rabbi of Dresden

who was a delegate, objected to the stand of the Conference that the use of Hebrew was 'desirable' but not 'legally essential' in the conducting of a Jewish service.

"Frankel had previously maintained that the conferences should be guided in their decisions by what he called 'the sentiment of the people.' As he described it, this seemed to many of the Reformers to be identical with practically all of Orthodox law. The leading Reformers could hardly agree with him since, to their way of thinking, the real 'sentiment of the people' demanded a change from Orthodoxy and the adjustment of Judaism to the needs of the changing times.

"Because of this conflict of ideas, Frankel finally withdrew from the Brunswick sessions and joined with others in the formation of a Conservative movement. He later became the head of its rabbinical seminary at Breslau.

"While Conservatism refused to modify basic Orthodox law, it proceeded to adopt some of the outward changes introduced by Reform, such as maintaining order during worship and sermon-preaching in the language of the country. These minor reforms satisfied those Jews who wanted some improvements in religious practices but objected to more fundamental changes. Hence, Conservatism attracted many who otherwise would probably have joined with Reform."

Reason #6—The Weaknesses of European Reform. "It seems to me," commented Father, "that there must have been certain weaknesses within European Reform itself that contributed to its own failure."

Great-Grandfather smiled. "There's no doubt about it," he said. "Certainly it never succeeded in becoming a truly unified or well-organized movement. European Reform failed to produce a complete religious platform upon which all of its leaders could agree. It did not even state officially that the whole of Jewish law was no longer binding upon the modern Jew. And, although the rabbinical conferences and synods did eventually reach decisions on a number of important Jewish beliefs and practices, all too little publicity was given to these and many temples continued to adopt their own independent programs of reforms.

"Moreover, the European movement possessed no unifying, permanent organization, either of congregations or rabbis. It wasn't until 1929, for instance, that many Reform congregations of Germany began using a common prayer book.

"Meanwhile Reform also began to suffer from loss of leadership, both lay and rabbinical. The restrictions which the governments of Europe had placed upon the Jews and the difficulties they encountered in achieving full citizenship discouraged many German Jews from remaining in their fatherland. Thus, beginning

EUROPEAN REFORM DEVELOPMENTS—FROM 1815

Important Historical Events	Happenings in Jewish Life	Developments in European Reform
1815—Defeat of Napoleon at Waterloo	1815—Reintroduction of restrictions against Jews in many sections of Europe	1818—Dedication of the Hamburg Temple 1820—Opening of a branch temple at Leipzig 1823—Government stops Berlin Reform services
1830—Successful revolution in France		1832—Zunz's *The Jewish Sermon* published 1838—Start of Geiger-Tiktin affair (to 1854) 1841—Hamburg prayer book controversy 1842—Dedication of the West London Synagogue of British Jews. Organization of the Frankfort Reform Society (to 1845) 1844—Brunswick Rabbinical Conference 1845—Frankfort Rabbinical Conference
	1846—Removal of the final restrictions against French Jewry	1846—Breslau Rabbinical Conference
1848—Unsuccessful revolutions in many parts of Europe	1859—Jews of northern Italy emancipated 1867—Emancipation of Austrian Jews	1869—Leipzig Synod
1870—Franco-Prussian War	1871—Completion of the emancipation of Italian Jews. Removal of last restrictions from English Jewry 1879—Beginning of anti-Semitic political parties 1881—Start of Russian pogroms	1871—Augsburg Synod 1872—Founding of the Liberal Rabbinical Seminary in Berlin
1894—Beginning of the Dreyfus Affair (to 1906)	1896—Judaism recognized as a legal religion in Hungary 1897—Formation of the World Zionist Organization	1899—Formation of the Union of Liberal Rabbis in Germany 1903—Founding of the Union Israélite Liberale in Paris

with the defeat of Napoleon in 1815 and continuing beyond the unsuccessful revolutions of 1848, increasing numbers of German Jews made their way to the United States. With them came the early leaders-to-be of the American Reform movement—rabbis like Max Lilienthal, Isaac Mayer Wise, David Einhorn, Samuel Adler, Bernhard Felsenthal, Samuel Hirsch, Kaufmann Kohler, and many others. Since Germany was the foremost center of European Reform, their emigration hurt the movement."

What Happened to Reform in Europe? As Great-Grandfather concluded, the family remained silent for a moment. Then Betty spoke up. "Well," she asked, "what finally happened to Reform Judaism in Europe? Did it go out of existence?"

"Oh, no," Great-Grandfather vigorously replied. "It still continued to grow, but very slowly. In England, for instance, a Jewish Religious Union was organized in 1902 with Claude G. Montefiore as its president. It was created to win back to Judaism those who had grown indifferent to the faith and was originally supported by both the Orthodox and Reform groups. But when it introduced Saturday afternoon services conducted almost entirely in English, using choir and organ, and seating men and women together, the Orthodox withdrew. The organization adopted a new name, 'The Jewish Religious Union for the Advancement of Liberal Judaism.' It established a Reform congregation, which within twenty-five years became the largest congregation in all England, having its own prayer book, conducting special services on Sunday, and permitting women to officiate at worship.

"In France, Reform made little headway. Although preaching in French was introduced in 1831 and Confirmation exercises ten years later, it was not until 1903 that the 'Union Israélite Liberale'—'The Union for Liberal Judaism'—was formed and it eventually built a temple in Paris. The congregation produced its own prayer book and, in addition to regular Sabbath services, conducted Sunday morning worship.

"Greater advances were made in Germany. In 1872, a seminary for the training of rabbis along Reform lines was founded in Berlin, and the

Claude G. Montefiore

'Union of the Liberal Rabbis of Germany' was organized in 1899 to establish common Reform beliefs and practices. Finally, in 1929, a 'union prayer book' for German Liberal congregations was adopted.

"But an indication of the European movement's failure to carry out a complete Reform program," Great-Grandfather disclosed, "is shown in this comment made by Dr. David Philipson, a leading American Reform rabbi, after his visit in 1928 to a Berlin Reform synagogue. 'Judging by the American standard of Reform,' he wrote, 'the German Reform service was Conservative if not Orthodox. The services were conducted almost entirely in Hebrew. The women were seated by themselves in the gallery, and the men worshipped with covered heads.' "

On to America! "I can see now why Reform developed so much more fully in America," Father commented. "Our government never questioned the rights of Jewish citizens nor did it interfere in matters of religion. Anti-Semitism as an organized movement was extremely ineffective and the Orthodox were not as strongly entrenched here as they had been in Europe. . . ."

"American Reform, too, has always enjoyed excellent leadership and good organization," Mother added, "and the liberal spirit of America must have prompted Jews to demand more far-reaching reforms

of Judaism than that offered by Conservatism."

"You're both right," nodded Great-Grandfather. "But suppose now we take a look at what really happened to Reform in the United States."

Betty was enthusiastic. "Well, it's about time!" she declared. "I've been wondering whether we were *ever* going to get to America. . . ."

QUESTIONS FOR DISCUSSION

1. What are the principal factors that contributed to Reform's failure in Europe?
2. In comparison with the situation in Europe, why was America so favorable to the development of Reform?
3. Why was the Orthodox opposition to Reform so effective in Europe?
4. How did political reaction and anti-Semitism hinder the growth of European Reform?
5. What factors were responsible for the rise of the Conservative movement?
6. How has American Reform attempted to overcome some of the inner weaknesses of the movement in Europe?

SUGGESTED   ACTIVITIES

1. Write an account of a day's happenings for a diary as though you were: (a) a Jew in Russia in the 1880's, or (b) a French Jew living through the Dreyfus Affair.
2. Prepare a map of Europe showing the political developments that af-

fected the Jews of various countries after the defeat of Napoleon.

3. (a) Invite the rabbi of a Conservative congregation to discuss the principles of Conservative Judaism, or (b) visit a Conservative synagogue and note the differences and similarities between its worship and that of Reform and Orthodoxy.

ADDITIONAL READINGS FOR PUPILS

FEUER, LEON I. and AZRIEL EISENBERG, *Jewish Literature Since the Bible, II,* pp. 236-238.

GOLUB, JACOB S. and ALAN S. GREEN, *A Short History of the Jews, III,* pp. 22-25.

LEVINGER, LEE J., *A History of the Jews in the United States,* pp. 212-213, 357-360.

LURIE, ROSE G., *The Great March, II,* pp. 202-204.

References for the Teacher

COHON, BERYL D., *Reform Judaism, Essays by Alumni of the Hebrew Union College,* "Conservative and Reconstructionist Judaism As Seen by a Reform Rabbi," pp. 107-121.

ELBOGEN, ISMAR, *A Century of Jewish Life,* Book 1, Chap. 1, "Emancipation in Central and Western Europe"; Book 2, Chap. 1, "Antisemitism as a Political Movement"; Chap. 2, "Antisemitism in Western Europe"; Chap. 3, "The Jews of Russia under Alexander III"; Book 3, Chap. 2, "Theodor Herzl and Political Zionism."

Jewish Encyclopedia, "Zacharias Frankel," Vol. 5, pp. 482-484.

MARCUS, JACOB R., *The Rise and Destiny of the German Jew,* Chap. 3, "The Origin of Anti-Semitism."

PHILIPSON, DAVID, *The Reform Movement in Judaism,* Chap. 13, "The Latest Developments in Europe."

ROTH, CECIL, *A Bird's-Eye View of Jewish History,* Chap. 29, "Anti-Semitism and the New Diaspora"; Chap. 30, "A New World."

SACHAR, ABRAM L., *A History of the Jews,* Chap. 24, "The Russian Jewish Nightmare"; Chap. 26, "The Revival of Anti-Semitism"; Chap. 27, "Zionism."

SCHWARTZMAN, SYLVAN D., *Reform Judaism in the Making,* Chap. 9, "Why European Reform Failed."

Universal Jewish Encyclopedia, "Judaism in America (Conservative Judaism)," Vol. 6, pp. 243-245; "Dreyfus Case," Vol. 3, pp. 596-599.

10. A LETTER FROM AMERICA, 1868

Why German Jews Came to the United States. The Friedberg family were seated in the living-room waiting for Great-Grandfather to tell them about the early days of Reform in America.

Betty broke the silence. "It certainly will be good to get back to the United States," she said with a sigh. "Some of those German names were awfully hard to remember . . . Leipzig . . . Augsburg . . . Breslau. . . ."

Father ventured a comment. "It's easy to see why many German Jews wanted to come to America," he observed. "They probably left Europe for some of the very reasons that prevented the growth of Reform."

"That's true," Great-Grandfather asserted, "but the main reason was the generally unfavorable attitude toward the Jews. Our people found very little real democracy in Europe and rarely enjoyed complete citizenship. They were discriminated against in business, government, and social life. In contrast, the United States was one of the few nations in which Jews were truly emancipated. Hence, this country offered Reform leaders their greatest opportunity to promote a modern form of Judaism."

Great-Grandfather Produces a Letter. "But let's see for ourselves what Jews of those days were thinking," said Great-Grandfather as he reached into his inner coat pocket and brought out an old, badly-worn envelope. "Here is a letter from a German friend of Father's who had come to America several years before we did," he explained. "Even as a boy I was greatly impressed with its contents. In fact, it possibly influenced our family to immigrate to the United States, and perhaps that's why I've saved it all these years."

He glanced down at the envelope. "It's post-marked December 5, 1868, and was mailed from Cincinnati, Ohio. Now listen. This is what our friend Nathan wrote."

As Great-Grandfather started to read, Betty could see from the many closely-written sheets that this was going to be a long letter.

The Voyage to America

December 5, 1868

Dear Jacob:

I have not forgotten my promise to write to you from America, but it has taken me some time to become accustomed to my new life, and particularly to learn the English language and American ways. Now that I have been here almost a year, I feel that I can give you a good report of life in the United States.

But let me begin with the voyage. We left Hamburg aboard a small boat which was terribly overcrowded with hundreds of German immigrants. Each cabin, normally accommodating two passengers at most, held as many as a dozen. The food was very bad; our meals consisted of a bowl of watery soup and a crust of bread three times a day throughout the two-months' trip. But what we feared most was the outbreak of some dread disease. However, our prayers for a safe voyage were answered and we landed in good physical condition at immigration headquarters in New York harbor.

I was amazed by the size of New York. Would you believe that many of the streets are actually paved! Such tall buildings and so busy a city with manufacturing and commerce! Why, there are even telegraph connections between New York and the rest of the United States.

Some of my fellow travelers decided to remain in New York and work in the garment factories, but I made up my mind to settle in the West. You can imagine how exciting it was to ride the steam-train all the way to the Ohio Valley. Cincinnati, which was my destination, numbers some 5,000 Jews and is the oldest western Jewish community. It was here that I began earning my living as a peddler, carrying a small supply of goods in a knapsack and selling them to farmers in the area.

The German Jew at Home in America

As I came to speak English more fluently and learned my merchandise, I started to make a better livelihood. But what I enjoyed most of all was the complete freedom of this country. Here the Jew is considered the equal of his Christian neighbor. Many of our people who settled in the United States earlier are highly-regarded citizens of their communities. Some have been elected to serve in state legislatures, and I have heard that two Jews helped nominate Abraham Lincoln for the Presidency. During the recent Civil War more than 10,000 of our brethren fought in both armies and many of them rose to high rank; some even became generals. In America, we also have a number of Jewish judges and government officials, all greatly respected by the people.

You can't imagine the peace and security we enjoy in this blessed land. Wherever the Jew has settled he has been kindly received. It often happens that I must spend nights away from home but I am treated by the hospitable farmers as though I were a member of their own families.

During the past year I managed to save enough money to open a small general merchandise shop in downtown Cincinnati. If business goes well perhaps it may grow into a large store like those which some of our brethren have already established.

I can hear you saying, "Tell me about American Jewish life," and knowing of your great interest in these matters, I will write you what I know.

There are almost 200,000 Jews living in the United States and well over half originate from Germany. We are scattered from New York all the way to California, but the largest centers of Jewish population are located in the East. New York has the greatest number, about 65,000, and Philadelphia, the next largest. We also have several old Jewish settlements in the South, like Charleston and Savannah.

Wherever our people reside they have their own synagogues, B'nai B'rith lodges, and charities. A number of our boys and girls attend universities, and plan to enter the medical, legal, and teaching professions. Today, the manufacturing of clothing is our largest industry; for, with the demand for uniforms during the Civil War, many of our people started their own clothing factories. A well-known Jewish firm is that of the Hart Brothers of Chicago. But we are also prominently represented in other occupations. Nelson Morris is becoming one of the leading American meat packers. Lazarus Straus runs a thriving pottery business and Brentano conducts a very important publishing house. Famous Jewish bankers include Kuhn, Loeb and Company, Hallgarten and Company, the Speyer Company, the Seligman brothers, and Henry Greenebaum.

THE BEGINNINGS OF AMERICAN REFORM

What about the Reform movement in the United States? Reform had its beginnings in Charleston, South Carolina. There, as far back as 1824, forty-seven members of the Beth Elohim Congregation petitioned the synagogue trustees to change the ritual. Influenced by news of reforms then being introduced in Germany, these members asked that important Jewish prayers be read or repeated in English, that an English sermon be delivered each week, and the lengthy Orthodox service be shortened. These improvements, they maintained, would enable the whole congregation to understand and enjoy the service more thoroughly.

When their petition was rejected, twelve members left the congregation and organized the "Reform Society of Israelites." By July of 1826 their membership had increased to more than fifty. Their form of worship included English as well as Hebrew prayers,

At the right is a picture of the old synagogue of Congregation Beth Elohim in Charleston, S.C. Reform Judaism in the United States had its beginning here. This building was destroyed by fire in 1838. The present temple building is shown above.

hymns in English, a shorter ritual, and fewer Orthodox ceremonies. They likewise denied all belief in the coming of a Messiah and the resurrection of the dead. They even provided for instrumental music during services, and the congregation worshipped with uncovered heads.

Unfortunately, the new congregation lasted only a few years. The strong opposition of Charleston Jewry coupled with lack of rabbinical leadership contributed to its failure, and many of the members rejoined the Beth Elohim Congregation.

In 1836, a new rabbi, Gustav Poznanski, became the spiritual leader of the Beth Elohim Congregation. Coming originally from Hamburg where he had been influenced by the reforms of the Hamburg Temple, Rabbi Poznanski determined to introduce a more modern form of Judaism in Charleston. When the synagogue burned down in 1838 and the congregation was planning to erect another, thirty-eight members joined Rabbi Poznanski in urging that an organ be installed in the new building. Orthodox members immediately objected and the controversy had to be decided by the Charleston courts. After three years, the rabbi and his followers received a favorable verdict, and the new synagogue, dedicated in 1841, was constructed with an organ. Two years later, again after a bitter struggle with the Orthodox, the congregation eliminated the extra days of the Jewish holidays. From then on, the Beth Elohim Congregation gradually developed into a full-fledged Reform temple.

REFORM SOCIETIES AND NEW CONGREGATIONS

For a while, Charleston had the only Reform congregation in the United States. All other synagogues were conducted along Orthodox lines with slight modifications of worship. Several Reform societies were soon organized and these developed into new Reform congregations in Baltimore, New York, Philadelphia, and Chicago.

In Baltimore, in April of 1842, a group of young Jewish men formed the Har Sinai Society, and used the Hamburg Temple prayer book in worship. Thus, the Har Sinai Congregation of Baltimore became the first American temple to be organized right from the start as a Reform congregation.

In 1845, the Emanu-El Congregation of New York was founded. It, too, had its origin as a Reform society. By the time the congregation had been in existence ten years it had already published its own prayer book, accepted the use of the organ, and introduced the Confirmation ceremony. All extra days of the Jewish holidays and the wearing of the talis were likewise eliminated at this time. In 1858 the membership agreed to worship with uncovered heads.

Albany, New York, established the next Reform temple in 1850 under the leadership of Rabbi Isaac Mayer Wise, a great leader of American Reform

Judaism. This same Rabbi Wise today serves a great Cincinnati congregation which became Reform in 1854.

In Philadelphia, Reform met with considerable opposition, for this was a great center of Orthodoxy under the leadership of Isaac Leeser, rabbi of Mikveh Israel Congregation and editor of *The Occident,* one of the most widely-read American-Jewish periodicals. For several years, a number of Jewish young men organized in a Reform society had tried to establish a congregation but without success. Finally, in 1856, the Reform society merged with the Keneseth Israel Congregation which had already shown interest in changing its form of worship, and as a result, the first Reform synagogue in Philadelphia came into existence.

In Chicago, too, a society was responsible for the formation of a Reform congregation. Several members of the Orthodox Anshe Ma-ariv Synagogue of Chicago had become dissatisfied with its practices and organized a Reform society. On April 17, 1858, at the first public session of the group, the members called upon Orthodox Judaism to eliminate its many out-of-date practices and make its services more understandable to modern Jews. Two years later, under the leadership of Rabbi Bernhard Felsenthal, the society became the Sinai Reform Congregation. In the preamble to its constitution, the new congregation adopted the following program of reforms: services shall be made thoroughly understandable and shall feature a regular sermon in English; the congregation shall provide modern Jewish religious education for the young; the congregation shall abolish all outlived Jewish laws, customs and practices, and shall substitute for them others more in keeping with modern American Jewish life.

Reform Judaism has already spread to many other communities of the United States. I am told that there are now Reform temples in Cleveland, Louisville, Milwaukee, Richmond, St. Louis, Boston, Memphis, Nashville, Detroit, Pittsburgh, and scores of other cities. Many more Orthodox congregations are gradually revising their services and introducing other reforms. As yet, there is no indication of any Conservative movement arising in the United States.

COMING: A UNIFIED REFORM MOVEMENT

Among Reform leaders today there is considerable talk of organizing a union of congregations. As early as 1848 Rabbi Isaac Mayer Wise proposed the idea, but nothing came of it. Now, however, there is much greater interest in bringing all Reform congregations into a single organization that will promote the development of the movement. Perhaps this time some plan will be adopted.

We are also confident that America will soon have its own seminary for the training of rabbis. Thus far all American Reform leaders have had to come from Europe. We hope, however, to be able to educate American-trained rabbis who are well acquainted with the ideas and spirit of this country. Once before, in 1855, the attempt to establish a school was made by the same Rabbi Wise when he opened Zion College in Cincinnati and enrolled fourteen students. He expected some of them would become rabbis. Unfortunately, he was forced to close the institution for lack of support, but there are many today who feel that the time is ripe for another attempt.

Meanwhile, Rabbi Wise has also been anxious to create a permanent organization of American rabbis to guide the development of Judaism in the United States. His early attempt in 1848–1849 did not succeed and a second effort on his part in 1855 also failed. In that year a conference of Orthodox and Reform rabbis as well as a few laymen was held in Cleveland and one of its decisions called upon Jews to practice their religion according to the teachings of the Talmud. Leading Reform congregations in the eastern part of the United States immediately objected and a split developed within the ranks of the American Reform movement, with the West defending the Cleveland decision and the East attacking it. Rabbi Wise, therefore, has had to postpone further attempts at organizing American Reform rabbis into a united body, but it will probably be achieved in the not too far distant future.

It now looks as if America will some day see a union of Reform congregations, a Reform seminary, and, perhaps, a permanent rabbinical conference.

I know that this has been a long letter, but I hope that it will make up for my delay in writing to you. I am wondering whether you plan to come to America; if so, please make Cincinnati your home. I have many good connections here and I am sure that I will be able to assist you.

Meanwhile, I send you my affectionate greetings.

Your friend,
(signed) *Nathan*

AMERICAN REFORM DEVELOPMENTS—TO 1869

Major European Reform Events	Reform Developments in America
1823—The government ends Reform services in Berlin	
	1824—Organization of the Charleston Reform Society
1838—Beginning of the Geiger-Tiktin affair (to 1854)	
1841—Hamburg Temple prayer book controversy	1841—Building of the Charleston temple with an organ
1842—Dedication of the West London Synagogue of British Jews. Organization of the Frankfort Reform Society	1842—Organization of the Har Sinai Reform Society in Baltimore
1844—Brunswick Rabbinical Conference	1844—Arrival of Max Lilienthal in the United States
1845—Frankfort Rabbinical Conference	1845—Formation of the Emanu-El Congregation in New York
1846—Breslau Rabbinical Conference	1846—Holding of the first Confirmation in the United States. Isaac M. Wise comes to America
1848—Beginning of large-scale emigration from Germany as a result of the unsuccessful revolution	
	1850—Formation of a Reform congregation in Albany
	1854—Founding of *The Israelite* by Wise
	1855—Adoption of Reform by 2 Cincinnati congregations completed. Holding of the Cleveland Conference. Opening of Zion College. Arrival of David Einhorn in the United States
	1856—Keneseth Israel Congregation of Philadelphia adopts Reform
	1857—Wise publishes his *Minhag America* prayer book
	1858—Formation of the Chicago Sinai Reform Society
1869—Leipzig Synod	1869—Philadelphia Rabbinical Conference

Betty Looks at a Picture. "That was a mighty full letter," Father commented as Great-Grandfather refolded the pages and put them back in the envelope, "but it certainly presents a thorough description of the early days of Reform in America."

"From what your father's friend wrote," Mother declared, "it becomes even clearer that here Reform met few of the conditions that had hindered its growth in all of Europe."

"In fact," added Father, "American Reform seems about ready to develop strong and unified organization."

Betty broke in. "Who was this Rabbi Wise that was mentioned so frequently in the letter?"

"A great American Reform organizer," Great-Grandfather answered. He rose and walked to the book-shelf from which he took down a small photograph album. "Here," he said, handing it to Betty, "are pictures of some of the early Reform leaders in this country."

Betty flicked open its covers to the first picture. The name beneath it read:

RABBI MAX LILIENTHAL

"Rabbi Max Lilienthal," she repeated. "Who was he?"

"Suppose we let him speak for himself," was Great-Grandfather's surprising answer. . . .

1. How did Jewish conditions in the America of the 1860's compare with those in Europe?
2. What factors present in America contributed to the growth of the Reform movement?
3. How did Reform originate in the United States?
4. What changes in traditional practices did the early American Reform movement introduce?
5. How was American Reform attempting to avoid the weaknesses of the movement in Europe?
6. What are the differences between the American Reform movement in the 1860's and the present day?

1. Prepare a map of the United States showing the important Reform developments in America up to the middle of the 1860's.
2. Write and present a radio drama dealing with the development of the Charleston Reform congregation.
3. Prepare a brief history of the founding of your congregation if it was originally established as Reform. If it became Reform after its founding, describe the circumstances that led it to become Reform.

ALOFSIN, DOROTHY, *The Stream of Jewish Life,* pp. 12-28.

GOLUB, JACOB S. and ALAN S. GREEN, *A Short History of the Jews, III,* pp. 47-50.

LEVINGER, LEE J., *A History of the Jews in the United States,* pp. 13-15, 175-189, 192-203, 213-217.

SOLOFF, MORDECAI I., *How the Jewish People Lives Today,* Chap. XVI, pp. 202-207.

References for the Teacher

ELBOGEN, ISMAR, *A Century of Jewish Life,* Book 1, Chap. 4, "The Jews in the New World," pp. 114-131.

Jewish Encyclopedia, "Judaism in America," Vol. 1, pp. 513-514.

MASSERMAN, PAUL and MAX BAKER, *The Jews Come to America,* Chap. 8, "The German Jews"; "The Reform Movement," Chap. 10, pp. 172-177.

PHILIPSON, DAVID, *The Reform Movement in Judaism,* "Reform in the United States," Chap. 12, pp. 329-339.

REZNIKOFF, CHARLES and URIAH Z. ENGELMAN, *The Jews of Charleston,* pp. 113-150, 200-207 (development of Reform in Charleston).

SCHWARTZMAN, SYLVAN D., *Reform Judaism in the Making,* Chap. 10, "Reform in the America of 1871."

Universal Jewish Encyclopedia, "Judaism in America (Reform Judaism)," Vol. 6, pp. 240-241.

11. THE FAMILY MEETS SOME AMERICAN REFORM LEADERS

A Picture Speaks for Itself! Betty took a second look at the picture of Rabbi Max Lilienthal and then she passed the photograph album to Mother and Father.

"I still want to know," she repeated, "who Rabbi Max Lilienthal was and what he had to do with Reform Judaism in America."

"Suppose we let each picture speak for itself," Great-Grandfather proposed.

"What do you mean?" Mother asked.

"Just this. . . ." Great-Grandfather continued talking but now he spoke with a heavy German accent. "I want to introduce myself," he said with a bow, "I am Rabbi Max Lilienthal, one of the first European Reform rabbis to come to the United States."

The family laughed. Great-Grandfather was quite good in his imitation and they began to understand what he had meant by "letting the pictures speak for themselves."

Rabbi Max Lilienthal (1815–1882). The family quieted down and Great-Grandfather went on. "As Max Lilienthal," he continued, "let me tell you something about myself.

"To begin with I must explain that I came to America as the result of an unfortunate experience in Russia. Born in Germany in 1815 and graduated from the University of Munich, I went to the Russian city of Riga at the age of twenty-four to become principal of a newly-established school for Jewish youth. I had been there only a year when the government appealed for my assistance with their educational program for Russian Jewry.

"The Russian people under the Czars had not experienced the freedoms of the French Revolution. Russia was still very much a part of the Middle Ages with its feudal system and mistreatment of Jews. Russian Jews were forced to live in only one section of the country called 'The Pale of Jewish Settlement.' The gov-

Max Lilienthal

ernment seized Jewish boys of twelve years of age and upward to serve in the army for a twenty-five-year period, and in their absence from home it made every effort to convert them to Christianity. Russian Jews were not permitted to employ Christian servants, erect synagogues near churches, or publish any Hebrew book without the approval of the government.

"But in 1840 the government announced a new policy toward the Jews. It promised them full citizenship if they would learn the Russian language and adopt Russian ways. The government pledged its assistance by opening special schools for Jewish children where they would be taught Russian as well as Jewish subjects. At the time I did not suspect that the corrupt officials had adopted this scheme to undermine Jewish education and make it easier to convert young Jews to Christianity.

"But the Russian Jews were suspicious of the government's motives because of past mistreatment, and they refused to send their children to these schools. Russian officials now called upon me to convince the Jews that these schools would aid them in obtaining liberty. They reasoned that if a fellow Jew appealed to them our people might cooperate, and again I was assured that the Russian government was sincere in its offer to emancipate its Jewry. I believed the story, and I traveled about the country speaking in favor of the plan.

"At first I met with some success in convincing prominent Jews to lend their support. Gradually, however, I found that I was distrusted and considered an 'agent' of the Russian government, and by 1842, I realized that my task was hopeless. Later, to my shame, I discovered the real purpose for which these schools were intended—to convert Jews to Christianity. Angered at the deceit of the government, I immediately left the country. In 1844 I sailed for America to begin life anew.

"I made my home in New York where I served as rabbi of several Orthodox synagogues for six years, and in 1846 conducted the first Confirmation service in the United States. Because of my Reform ideas I was opposed by many Orthodox congregants and temporarily gave up the rabbinate. It was while I was in New York that I first met Isaac Mayer Wise who had just arrived from Europe. I urged him to carry on the struggle for Reform Judaism

in America and we became lifelong friends.

"In 1854 I was appointed New York correspondent for Rabbi Wise's newspaper, *The Israelite,* and a year later, at his insistence, I moved to Cincinnati to become his associate editor and the rabbi of Bene Israel Congregation. In my congregational work and my writings I continually fought against a Judaism which refused to adjust to the needs of modern American Jews.

"When, in 1875, Rabbi Wise established the Hebrew Union College, the first rabbinical seminary in America to carry on permanently, I immediately volunteered my services and became its professor of history and literature."

Great-Grandfather filled in the rest of the story. "This pioneer of American Reform Judaism, Max Lilienthal, died in Cincinnati in 1882 at the age of sixty-seven."

Rabbi David Einhorn (1809–1879). "Now turn to the next picture in the album," Great-Grandfather called to Betty, "and let's meet Rabbi David Einhorn."

She did as Great-Grandfather asked and held the picture up for all to see.

"What role did he play in the development of Reform Judaism in America?" questioned Father.

"Suppose we also let Rabbi Einhorn speak for himself," Great-Grandfather declared.

"I am now David Einhorn," he

David Einhorn

began, "and like so many other early American Reform rabbis, I immigrated to the United States because I hated Europe's discrimination against our people and was discouraged by the slow progress of the Reform movement. And, because I had to fight so hard in Europe for the right to express my Reform beliefs, I was determined that in this free country I would never compromise them. That is why I was widely known as the leader of the 'radical Reformers' in America.

"I was born in Germany in 1809 and received excellent Jewish training at the Talmudic School of Fürth so that at the age of seventeen I was ordained a rabbi. Then, in a little while, eager to obtain a general education, I attended several Bavarian universities.

"Although I had been the favorite pupil of my teachers at the Talmudic School, my interest in securing a college education immediately turned them against me. Now they denounced me as an 'unbeliever,' and for ten years they did everything they could to prevent my election as rabbi of any congregation. When, for example, the Wellhausen congregation invited me to become its rabbi, my former teachers influenced the Bavarian government to prohibit me from serving.

"Their narrowness and hatred of everything modern made me all the more determined to modernize our religion, and even though I was destined to suffer many disappointments because of my liberal beliefs, I remained a champion of Reform. At last, in 1842, I obtained my first pulpit in Hoppstädten, a small German community, where I began my active program of Reform.

"I was particularly interested in the German rabbinical conferences of 1844 to 1846, and personally participated in the last two. At the Frankfort Conference I urged that prayers in the German language be incorporated into the Jewish service, and that prayers for a return from 'exile' be abolished. At the Breslau Conference in 1846 I was appointed chairman of a committee to study and recommend revisions of Jewish dietary laws, and throughout all of the meetings I advocated equal religious rights for Jewish women.

"In 1847 I became the rabbi of a congregation in Mecklenburg-Schwerin only to become involved in a serious controversy with the Orthodox. I maintained that a child born to Jewish parents was automatically a Jew; therefore, I consented to bless an uncircumcised Jewish child in my synagogue. The Orthodox immediately accused me of violating the teachings of Judaism, and when my own members failed to support me, I resigned from the congregation.

"Another disappointment followed. Two months after I was elected rabbi of the Budapest Reform Congregation, the Orthodox opposition influenced the Austrian government to close the temple. Moreover, it refused to hear my appeal.

"Now, in 1855, at the age of forty-six I agreed to come to the United States and occupy the pulpit of the Har Sinai Congregation of Baltimore, the first temple organized from the start as Reform. Gradually I became recognized as leader of the Reform movement in the East. In fact, I headed a revolt of the eastern Reform rabbis against Isaac Mayer Wise who, in the interests of American Jewish unity, supported a resolution of the Cleveland Conference that the Talmud was binding upon the American Jew. While Wise hoped thereby to create harmony between both the Reform and Orthodox groups, I insisted that no matter what the cost we had to be honest in our Judaism and not accept as part of our Jewish law any ceremonial, practice or regulation that could not possibly be observed under modern conditions. To me, ceremonials and practices were only the outer teachings of our faith which 'had to change according to different stages of culture, national customs, industrial, social and civil conditions.'

" 'Jewish history,' I firmly maintained, 'proved that our religion changed many times to meet new conditions of Jewish life. The Talmud itself originated as one of those very changes, and the reinterpretation of the Bible which it accomplished enabled our people to exist under the most trying conditions of the Middle Ages. But now that we lived in a new age of freedom, the Talmud could no longer regulate our faith.'

"Such was my argument and people asked, 'What, then, is permanent in Judaism?' I replied, 'The inner or fundamental teachings of our religion—the Ten Commandments, belief in the One Eternal God, faith in the goodness that is in all men and in their right to equal happiness under equal laws, the belief that some day all mankind will find this happiness here on earth in a great Messianic Age. These are the Jewish teachings that cannot be altered or changed.'

"Isaac Mayer Wise, of course, subscribed to these general Reform principles. But where we disagreed was that he was willing to compromise with the Orthodox in order to gain their cooperation in the organization of American Jewish life. On the other hand, I felt that Reform could not and should not surrender its beliefs under any circumstances.

"This was the beginning of many public arguments with Rabbi Wise. I am afraid that I lost my patience with him and attacked him and his ideas vigorously. But he was also equally sharp in his opposition to me. To help spread my views, I soon began publishing a German-language magazine, *Sinai*. Many people were influenced in my favor by some of its articles as well as by the prayer book I had written in 1858 which was being used by a growing number of congregations.

"I fought for my convictions on other issues as well. When the Civil War broke out in 1861, I spoke out boldly against slavery and those who supported it. Baltimore was very much pro-South in its sentiments, and rumors began to circulate that I might be lynched. My family and I were persuaded to find safety in Philadelphia. Later the Baltimore congregation invited me to return to the pulpit, but the letter which they sent infuriated me. Although they meant it for my own good, they wrote, 'It will be desirable . . . if, in the future, you will avoid any remarks, referring to the excitement of the day, from your pulpit.' I promptly sent them my resignation. When a congregational committee called upon me to reconsider my decision, I told them, 'I left Europe only to have the right of free speech. I will never obey such orders!'

"I then accepted the rabbinical post with Keneseth Israel Congregation of Philadelphia and continued my work in behalf of Reform. In 1866 I left Philadelphia to take a New York pulpit which, through a merger of synagogues, became the Beth-El Congregation. Three years later I helped prepare the first Reform statement of beliefs at the Philadelphia Rabbinical Convention.

"Like Isaac Mayer Wise, I, too, recognized the great need for an American rabbinical seminary, and while rabbi in New York, I tried unsuccessfully to establish one. Later I joined with Rabbi Wise in supporting the development of the Hebrew Union College by serving as chairman of its committee on the course of studies. For, as the years passed, our controversy over Reform Judaism had grown less violent."

Great-Grandfather now spoke for himself. "David Einhorn," he concluded, "died at the age of seventy, shortly after he retired from his New York pulpit. Because he had the courage to fight for his Reform beliefs and refused to compromise when he felt he was right, we honor him as one of the great founders of American Reform Judaism. In fact," Great-Grandfather pointed out, "he made a number of outstanding contributions to Reform's cause. Did you know, for instance, that his original prayer book serves as the basis of our own *Union Prayerbook?*"

Rabbi Isaac Mayer Wise (1819–1900). "I still want to hear about Rabbi Wise," Betty insisted.

"His picture is next," Great-Grandfather told her, and she turned the page of the album.

"I recognize him," said Mother, as Betty held the book aloft. "Yes, that's Isaac Mayer Wise."

"His picture is well known," Great-Grandfather said, "for he did most to develop the movement and was responsible for providing Reform Judaism with its excellent organization."

"Let the picture speak for itself," Betty reminded him.

"All right, then," declared Great-Grandfather, and he started to speak as if he were really Rabbi Wise. "I am now Isaac Mayer Wise, born on March 29, 1819, in the tiny village of Steingrub, Bohemia. At the age of four I began my Jewish studies with my father, a Hebrew teacher, and by the time I reached twelve, I had already made up my mind to become a rabbi.

"By 1842 I completed my Jewish training and thus at twenty-three was ordained a rabbi in Israel. The following year I was elected to serve a congregation in a small Bohemian town, but I had no patience with Europe's treatment of our people and I left with my wife and daughter for the United States.

"In order to earn a living in New York I had to tutor private pupils. It was there that I met Max Lilien-

Isaac M. Wise

thal who encouraged me to remain a rabbi and work for the cause of Reform Judaism.

"Shortly thereafter I was invited to become rabbi of the Beth El Congregation of Albany, New York. I promptly began a program of reforms. I trained a choir of men and women to render the music at the service, made it a custom to preach a weekly sermon, omitted some of the Hebrew prayers, and even changed a number of other synagogue practices. Of course, I met with opposition from some members of the congregation and was condemned by *The Occident* when word reached its Orthodox editor, Isaac Leeser, of Philadelphia.

"Serious trouble, however, broke out following my visit to Charleston, South Carolina. The Reform congregation there had been under attack by a Dr. Raphall and I accepted an invitation to debate against him. During the course of that debate I stated that I no longer believed in the coming of a Messiah or in the resurrection of the dead. Word of my remarks reached Albany and helped turn the president of my congregation against me. He now became a spokesman for the Orthodox element and sought to have me dismissed by the trustees, but was unsuccessful.

"Finally, at a highly irregular meeting of the congregation called by the president on September 5, 1850, I was discharged. However, my many friends persuaded me to officiate during the approaching High Holydays. When I entered the synagogue to conduct the Rosh Ha-shono service, I found my seat occupied by an Orthodox opponent. I stepped before the Ark to take out the Torah and the president of the congregation struck me. The synagogue broke into an uproar. Police had to be called to restore order and, to prevent further trouble, they closed the synagogue.

"Within a week my friends had organized the new Anshe Emeth Congregation, the fourth Reform congregation in America; and, in rented rooms on the upper floor of an ordinary building, I conducted the Yom Kippur services. Soon we purchased a synagogue building, installed an organ and instituted family pews in which men and women could sit together. Reform now made splendid progress in Albany.

"In September of 1853 I accepted the call to become rabbi of the Bene Yeshurun Congregation of Cincin-

nati. Although my new congregation was quite Orthodox, I was soon busy training a choir and having an organ installed. My sermons were so well received that the older congregation of the city, Bene Israel, asked me to become its rabbi. I declined the offer but consented to preach for the congregation every Saturday afternoon; and finally, in 1855, upon my recommendation, they selected as their rabbi, my good friend, Max Lilienthal.

"Gradually my Cincinnati congregation became one of America's leading Reform temples. I introduced the late Friday evening service which has become so popular with Reform congregations and cooperated in the writing of an American Reform prayer book in both English and German editions, the *Minhag America*, published in 1857 and adopted by congregations throughout the South and West.

"I carried on many duties beyond the confines of the congregation. For nearly fifty years I wrote, edited, and published an English weekly, *The Israelite*—renamed *The American Israelite* in 1875—and a German-language weekly, *Die Deborah*, for Jews who could not as yet read English fluently. In their pages I published my own novels, programs for Reform Judaism, attacks on prejudice and anti-Semitism, and unceasing appeals for the creation of a union of congregations, an American rabbinical seminary, and a permanent rabbinical organization. I also managed to travel to dozens of American cities dedicating new synagogues and spreading the message of Reform.

"The founding of a rabbinical seminary in the United States was one of my greatest ambitions. In October of 1854, I proposed that such a college be established in Cincinnati. 'Let us educate our ministers here in our own college, and we will soon have American ministers, American congregations,' I wrote in *The Israelite*. The following year we opened Zion College with fourteen students, but we were forced to close for lack of support.

"Naturally, I was disappointed by our failure but not discouraged, and I continued to agitate for a rabbinical seminary. Eventually my hopes rose when, on July 8, 1873, delegates representing twenty-eight congregations met in Cincinnati and organized the Union of American Hebrew Congregations whose first main objective was the establishment of a 'Hebrew Theological College.' At its initial meeting in Cleveland in 1874, the new Union of American Hebrew Congregations agreed to create the Hebrew Union College in Cincinnati. A short time after, I was elected to serve as its president, and on October 3, 1875, the Hebrew Union College opened its doors. By 1900, sixty-one of its graduates were already officiating at the principal American Reform temples.

"With the creation of our union of congregations and rabbinical seminary we lacked but one other organization to unify and strengthen our movement—a permanent conference of rabbis. Ever since I had come to the United States I urged its formation but our discussions for the purpose in 1848–1849 and 1855 were fruitless. Gradually I came to see the impossibility of having a single rabbinical conference for both Orthodox and Reform rabbis. In fact, in 1855, even our Reform rabbis were split into two opposing groups, for in that year the Cleveland Conference approved a resolution which declared that the Talmud was binding upon the American Jew. Rabbis of the East like David Einhorn of Baltimore strongly objected to this compromise measure and insisted that Reform stand by its principles. We of the West, however, saw the necessity for American Jewish unity even if it involved certain concessions to the Orthodox. No doubt some of the controversy was also caused by jealousy of my position of leadership. I recall one accusation that was made—'Rabbi Wise wants to be the Jewish Archbishop of American Israel.'

"During the next thirty-five years only three rabbinical meetings took place, but each, in turn, contributed toward the final organization of the Reform rabbinate. The rabbinical conference at Philadelphia in 1869 established the first principles of American Reform Judaism. The meeting in 1871 in Cincinnati inspired the formation of the Union of American Hebrew Congregations. In 1885, the Pittsburgh Conference adopted a complete platform for American Reform. The old quarrel between Reform leaders of East and West was being healed and a number of eastern Reform congregations had already joined the Union of American Hebrew Congregations.

"Finally, in 1889, I succeeded in organizing the Central Conference of American Rabbis in Detroit. The ninety rabbis who attended honored me with election as their first president, and each succeeding year the Conference reelected me."

Great-Grandfather concluded the story of Isaac Mayer Wise by saying, "His death came just as he had lived —in the midst of work for Reform Judaism. He had preached the morning sermon at Plum Street Temple in Cincinnati and, as he was meeting with his afternoon class at the Hebrew Union College, he suffered a stroke. At sundown on Monday, March 26, 1900, he passed away.

"Educator, author, lecturer, editor, organizer, and rabbi, Isaac Mayer Wise was the greatest of the early American Reform rabbis. He remained president of the Hebrew Union College and Central Conference of American Rabbis until the day of his death. It was Rabbi Wise who spread the message of Reform throughout the United States, and particularly in the West. Through

the pages of *The American Israelite,* hundreds of newspaper articles, meetings, visits, and addresses, he brought Reform to the attention of the people. And, by the creation of three vital organizations—the Union of American Hebrew Congregations, the Hebrew Union College, and the Central Conference of American Rabbis—he provided Reform with the strength and unity which it had lacked in Europe."

The family remained very quiet for they were greatly stirred by the story of Isaac Mayer Wise and his accomplishments.

Father finally broke the silence. "He was a remarkable leader," he said softly.

"One of the greatest in all of Jewish history," asserted Great-Grandfather.

Other Early Reform Leaders. "But let's not imagine," Great-Grandfather added hastily, "that Lilienthal, Einhorn, and Wise were the only early American Reform leaders. There are many others. . . ."

"For instance?" Mother asked.

Betty held up the next picture in Great-Grandfather's album.

"That's Samuel Adler," Great-Grandfather announced. "He lived from 1809 to 1891. Before coming to America in 1857, he had participated in the German rabbinical conferences. He served as rabbi of Temple Emanu-El of New York for nineteen years and was a man of action

MAP OF REFORM DEVELOPMENTS IN AMERICA

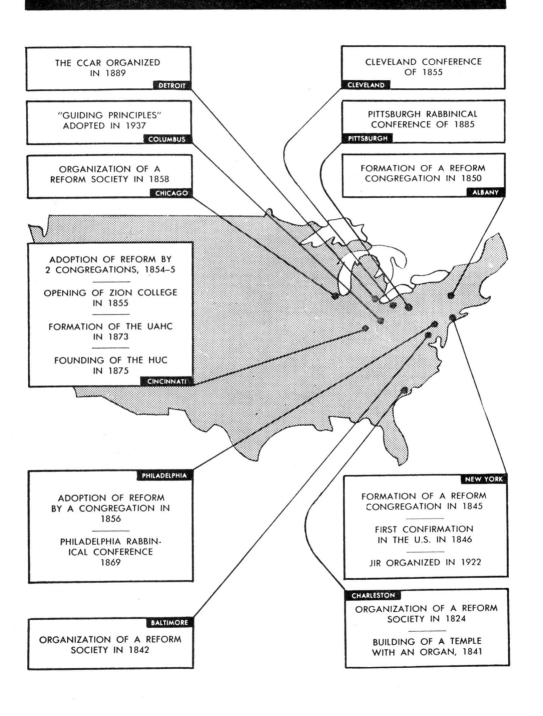

THE CCAR ORGANIZED
IN 1889

DETROIT

CLEVELAND CONFERENCE
OF 1855

CLEVELAND

"GUIDING PRINCIPLES"
ADOPTED IN 1937

COLUMBUS

PITTSBURGH RABBINICAL
CONFERENCE OF 1885

PITTSBURGH

ORGANIZATION OF A
REFORM SOCIETY IN 1858

CHICAGO

FORMATION OF A REFORM
CONGREGATION IN 1850

ALBANY

ADOPTION OF REFORM BY
2 CONGREGATIONS, 1854–5

OPENING OF ZION COLLEGE
IN 1855

FORMATION OF THE UAHC
IN 1873

FOUNDING OF THE HUC
IN 1875

CINCINNATI

PHILADELPHIA

NEW YORK

ADOPTION OF REFORM
BY A CONGREGATION IN
1856

PHILADELPHIA RABBIN-
ICAL CONFERENCE
1869

FORMATION OF A REFORM
CONGREGATION IN 1845

FIRST CONFIRMATION
IN THE U.S. IN 1846

JIR ORGANIZED IN 1922

CHARLESTON

ORGANIZATION OF A REFORM
SOCIETY IN 1824

BUILDING OF A TEMPLE
WITH AN ORGAN, 1841

BALTIMORE

ORGANIZATION OF A REFORM
SOCIETY IN 1842

as well as of great learning. It was Rabbi Adler who insisted upon equal religious rights for Jewish women and who fought for the improvement of Jewish religious education. Because of the great number of learned articles he wrote, he was also known as a distinguished scholar."

Betty turned the album page. "That's a picture of Bernhard Felsenthal, another early Reform leader," Great-Grandfather said, as he looked over her shoulder. "He was born in 1822 and died in 1908. He came from Germany in 1854 and became the first rabbi of the Sinai Reform Congregation of Chicago. His pamphlet, 'A Voice Calling in the Wilderness,' published in 1859, was the most widely-circulated appeal for Reform Judaism in his day. In it he upheld the right of modern Jews to modify all outgrown religious laws. He was also a prominent champion of Zionism and in 1896 in Chicago helped form the first Zionist society in the United States.

"Another leader," Great-Grandfather continued, "was Samuel Hirsch (1815–1889). There's his picture," he said, pointing to the album which Betty passed to Mother and Father. "Before coming to the United States he had already been recognized in Europe as one of its foremost Reform rabbis. In 1866 he received a call to occupy the pulpit of Keneseth Israel Congregation of Philadelphia, and he remained there until a year before his death. A great Reform thinker,

he was elected president of the Philadelphia Rabbinical Conference in 1869, and there presided over the first formulation of Reform's principles."

When Great-Grandfather Spoke with Rabbi Wise. "Tell me, Great-Grandfather," Betty asked, "did you know any of these rabbis personally?"

"Of course," he answered. "I knew Rabbis Wise and Lilienthal extremely well. After all, they were rabbis in Cincinnati, and that is where I made my home after I left Frankfort. I never will forget," he reminisced, "the afternoon in 1885 I spent with Rabbi Wise. It was just after he had returned from the famous Pittsburgh Rabbinical Conference. . . ."

"You actually met with Isaac Mayer Wise!" exclaimed Betty.

"Certainly."

"Well," Mother wanted to know, "what did you two talk about?"

"The Pittsburgh Rabbinical Conference."

It was Father who asked the next question. "What was that?"

"How did you happen to be discussing it with Rabbi Wise?" questioned Betty.

"And what did Rabbi Wise tell you?" Mother asked.

Great-Grandfather threw up his hands. "This Friedberg family can ask more questions!" he complained. "If you'll only wait a minute, I'll tell you all about it. . . ."

In connection with this chapter the class will want to see the filmstrip, "Isaac Mayer Wise: Master Builder of American Judaism," which may be secured through the Union of American Hebrew Congregations.

QUESTIONS FOR DISCUSSION

1. What conditions in Europe prompted the early Reformers to immigrate to America?

2. What were some problems facing the early Reformers in creating a Reform movement in America?

3. What was the contribution of David Einhorn to the development of American Reform Judaism?

4. What did Wise contribute to the Reform movement in the U.S.?

5. Why were there conflicts between some of the early American Reform leaders?

6. What beliefs, practices, and institutions of present-day Reform are the result of the work of the early American Reform leaders?

SUGGESTED ACTIVITIES

1. Conduct a debate on the subject: "*Resolved,* That Einhorn had the more correct view of Reform Judaism than Wise."

2. Write and present a dramatic sketch of the life of Max Lilienthal.

3. Create a newspaper article under the headline: "Reform Rabbis Organize Central Conference."

Additional Readings for Pupils

ALOFSIN, DOROTHY, *The Stream of Jewish Life,* pp. 12-46.

FEUER, LEON I. and AZRIEL EISENBERG, *Jewish Literature Since the Bible, II,* pp. 190-198.

KALISHER, BETTY, *Watchmen of the Night,* pp. 187-197.

LEVINGER, LEE J., *A History of the Jews in the United States,* pp. 194, 217-219, 225-238.

LURIE, ROSE G., *The Great March, II,* pp. 162-178.

SOLOFF, MORDECAI I., *How the Jewish People Lives Today,* pp. 150-160.

References for the Teacher

Jewish Encyclopedia, "Samuel Adler," Vol. 1, p. 199; "David Einhorn," Vol. 5, pp. 78-79; "Bernhard Felsenthal," Vol. 5, pp. 361-362; "Samuel Hirsch," Vol. 6, pp. 417-418; "Max Lilienthal," Vol. 8, pp. 86-87; "Isaac Mayer Wise," Vol. 12, pp. 541-542.

KOHLER, KAUFMANN, *Central Conference of American Rabbis Yearbook,* "David Einhorn, the Uncompromising Champion of Reform Judaism," Vol. 19, pp. 215-270.

MASSERMAN, PAUL and MAX BAKER, *The Jews Come to America,* pp. 177-201 (Isaac Mayer Wise).

MAY, MAX B., *Isaac Mayer Wise.*

PHILIPSON, DAVID, *Max Lilienthal, American Rabbi.*

——, *The Reform Movement in Judaism,* pp. 339-353 (early American Reform leaders).

SCHWARTZMAN, S. D., *Reform Judaism in the Making,* Chap. 11, "The Creators of American Reform."

Universal Jewish Encyclopedia, "Samuel Adler," Vol. 1, p. 97; "David Einhorn," Vol. 4, pp. 27-28; "Bernhard Felsenthal," Vol. 4, pp. 273-274; "Samuel Hirsch," Vol. 5, p. 379; "Max Lilienthal," Vol. 7, pp. 62-63; "I. M. Wise," Vol. 10, pp. 539-542.

12. REFORM GETS A SET OF PRINCIPLES

The Beginnings at Philadelphia, 1869. "Yes," repeated Great-Grandfather, "I never will forget that November afternoon when we sat together in Rabbi Wise's home. Isaac Mayer Wise had just returned from Pittsburgh where he and eighteen other Reform rabbis had been meeting."

The Friedberg family were waiting to hear the full story. Mother turned toward Great-Grandfather. "What," she asked, "was so unusual about this meeting? After all, this wasn't the first rabbinical conference that Reform had held."

"But," Great-Grandfather disclosed, "this was the first one to give Reform a complete set of principles."

"Aha!" exclaimed Betty, "Reform Judaism solves another problem in America! So we finally produced a common Reform program?"

"Correct," Great-Grandfather asserted. "Here in the United States

our movement created a platform which guided Reform Judaism for fifty-two years. But the Pittsburgh Platform really had its origin in the decisions of the Philadelphia Rabbinical Conference of 1869."

"What happened there?" Father wanted to know.

"It was in Philadelphia," Great-Grandfather answered, "that twelve Reform rabbis met and agreed on certain basic Reform beliefs."

"Won't you please tell us something about them?" Mother requested.

"Briefly," Great-Grandfather summarized, "the rabbis established four fundamental Reform principles. First, they said that as citizens of this country they no longer mourned the loss of Palestine, looked forward to a return to that land or the rebuilding of the old Temple. Secondly, they did not believe that after death the human body would ever be restored to life; rather, they felt that it was man's soul which returned to God. Thirdly, they maintained that the Jews were selected by God to make His teachings known to all mankind, and that being scattered throughout the world aided them in carrying out this mission more effectively. And finally, they stated that while they sought to preserve the Hebrew language, they also insisted that religious services be understandable to modern Jews.

"Not only did the Philadelphia Rabbinical Conference adopt these principles," Great-Grandfather went on, "but it boldly met the problem of Jewish divorce laws by declaring that Jews need no longer obtain a religious divorce. A civil divorce granted by the State and having the consent of both husband and wife was sufficient."

"So it took American Reform to settle the issue of the Jewish divorce, too," Father observed.

"Yes," said Great-Grandfather, "and the Conference also reaffirmed the decision of the European Reformers to accept a certificate of death issued by the State in permitting the 'Aguno' to remarry. . . ."

Great-Grandfather Reminisces. Betty broke in with a question. "How long after the Philadelphia meeting did the Pittsburgh Conference take place?"

"Sixteen years," he replied. "From November 16 to 18, 1885, nineteen rabbis gathered in Pittsburgh at the

Kaufmann Kohler

call of Rabbi Kaufmann Kohler, rabbi of Temple Beth-El of New York, and one of Reform's outstanding thinkers."

"And what were some of the things they discussed?" Father queried.

"That's precisely what I asked Rabbi Wise," Great-Grandfather stated. He started to recall the experience. "Let me see," he mused as he began reminiscing. . . .

*   *   *

"It was a brisk November afternoon in 1885 and we were sitting together in Rabbi Wise's study. Isaac Mayer Wise was excited about the results of the Pittsburgh Conference. 'A very important meeting, David,' Rabbi Wise assured me.

" 'What questions did you consider there, Rabbi Wise?' I asked him.

" 'The first problem,' he answered, 'was that of Sabbath observance.' "

The Question of Sabbath Observance. " 'Why was Sabbath observance an issue?' I asked.

" 'As you know, David,' he replied, 'modern business conditions have made it extremely difficult for Jews to keep Saturday as the Sabbath. As far back as 1866, I tried to meet the problem by introducing late Friday evening services. This enabled the people who had to work on Shabos to observe some part of the Sabbath in congregational worship.'

" 'I understand that there was an excellent response,' I remarked.

" 'But not with everybody. A number of congregations proposed Sunday services as a solution. In 1874, the Sinai Congregation of Chicago began holding services on Sunday in addition to regular Saturday worship. Their success in attracting large numbers of Jews to temple prompted other congregations to follow the example. Several rabbis began to suggest the transfer of the Jewish Sabbath to Sunday. But others were opposed even to Sunday services and warned that they would merely contribute to the non-observance of the Jewish Sabbath. This was one of the issues at the Pittsburgh Conference.'

" 'And what was the decision?'

" 'We agreed that for the sake of Jewish tradition and world-wide Jewish unity it was essential to keep Saturday as our Sabbath. But we also recognized that American business practices made it impossible for many Jews to attend Saturday worship. Therefore, while we refused to break with Jewish tradition, we resolved that there was nothing whatever in Judaism which prohibited the holding of a week-day service on Sunday.'

" 'That seems wise,' I told him. 'In this way the Conference followed Reform principles in building upon Jewish tradition and at the same time adjusting religious practice to modern conditions.' I paused a moment. Then I asked, 'Was that all the Conference accomplished?'

"Rabbi Wise handed me a sheet of paper. I noted that there were eight items listed on the page. 'Here,' he said, 'is our major achievement—the Pittsburgh Platform of Reform Judaism.'

"I started to glance over the page. 'Read them aloud,' Rabbi Wise called to me, 'one at a time.'

"I followed his request and read out the first principle."

" 'This first principle,' Rabbi Wise commented, 'established as the most

THE FIRST PLANK

Judaism and God

1.

WE recognize in every religion the attempt of men to discover God. However, we believe that Judaism presents the finest idea of God. As taught by our Bible, our rabbis and our great thinkers, we Jews, in spite of persecution, have preserved this God-idea for all mankind.

important element of Judaism the belief in the one, eternal, all-powerful God who demands righteousness from every individual. No other religion,' he insisted, 'presents such a complete idea of the one God. Jews have endured great suffering and persecution for the sake of preserving and transmitting this God-idea, and even today it remains Judaism's greatest teaching and the Jew's most important contribution to the religions of the world.'

"When he finished his remarks, I turned to the second article, and read it aloud":

THE SECOND PLANK

Jewish Teaching and Science

2.

THE Bible is the record of the Jewish people's experience as believers in the one God. While we hold that the Bible is vital for its great religious teachings, we recognize that portions of it contain legends from ancient times. We admit that these are only legendary and cannot, therefore, conflict with the discoveries of modern science.

" 'What was the purpose of this statement?' I questioned Rabbi Wise.

" 'This was our answer to one of modern religion's most troublesome problems,' he declared. 'For many years, scientists have been telling us that some of the Biblical stories about the beginnings of the world, the creation of man, and various miracles were not accurate. Ever since, fierce arguments have continued to rage between scientists and those religionists, both Christians and Jews, who consider the entire Bible the word of God and hence all of it absolutely true. . . .'

"I interrupted him to ask, 'With whom have you sided, Rabbi Wise?'

" 'I've opposed the viewpoint of the scientists,' he answered, 'but other Reform rabbis, like Einhorn and Kohler, have been convinced that the Bible could not have been handed down in its present form from God to Moses. They point to the many scribal errors in the text and contradictory teachings from different periods of Israel's early history that have been woven together. Some Biblical ideas, they contend, originated in very ancient times when people truly believed that the world was created in only seven days and that woman came from Adam's rib. But these accounts, they hold, merely express what early peoples believed and not actual happenings. As you can see from our platform, we finally agreed that they and the scientists are right in such matters.'

" 'How does this affect the religious value of the Bible?' I inquired.

" 'This certainly does not mean,' he quickly explained, 'that the Bible is not considered a great religious work. On the contrary, the Bible is still our most important source of religious inspiration and instruction. Furthermore,' he added, 'without it we would be unable to understand the development of Judaism, the Jew, and the many Jewish contributions to the religious beliefs of mankind.'

"I returned to the list of principles he had given me":

THE THIRD PLANK

Jewish Ceremonies and Laws

3.

MANY Biblical laws originated when our people lived principally in Palestine. Today, as citizens of other lands, Jews can no longer accept all of these laws. Nor can we continue to practice those ceremonies which are not in keeping with modern times. We accept as binding, therefore, only those Biblical laws that aid us to become better men and women, and only those ceremonies which are meaningful to modern Jews.

" 'At Pittsburgh,' Rabbi Wise pointed out, 'we had to decide which Biblical teachings were acceptable to Reform. We immediately recognized that it was impossible for us to observe many of the laws that had regulated Jewish life in Palestine.'

" 'Do you mean Biblical laws such as the observance of the Sabbatical year—every seventh year when land was not to be cultivated and debts were not to be collected?'

" 'Yes,' he answered, 'for now that we were citizens of many countries, such laws could not be put into effect. Likewise we could not accept any Biblical ceremonies which, because of the changed ideas and circumstances of modern Jewry, had become outmoded.'

" 'Like the daily practice of putting on the t'filin (two small black leather boxes containing Bible passages and worn on the head and arm)?'

" 'That's right,' he replied. 'We insist that ceremonies must have religious meaning for Jews of today.'

"I now read the next article of the Pittsburgh Platform":

THE FOURTH PLANK

Jewish Diet and Dress

4.

ALL Biblical and rabbinical laws regulating foods forbidden or permitted to Jews, ritual purity, and Jewish dress need no longer be obeyed. These laws do not contribute to the leading of a better life, nor are they in keeping with modern times.

" 'As you know,' Rabbi Wise explained, 'the Bible, Talmud, and other rabbinical writings regulate the types of food that Jews may or may not eat. These laws come under the heading of kashrus, keeping kosher.'

" 'I am familiar with some of the dietary laws,' I stated. 'There are kosher—ritually permissible—kinds of animals and fish that Jews may eat; there are others, however, that are prohibited. Animals that do not have split hooves and do not chew the cud, or fish without scales and fins are non-kosher and may not be eaten.'

" 'Correct!' asserted Rabbi Wise, 'and remember, too, that kosher animals must be ritually slaughtered by a *shochet*. He is the man who has been trained to kill animals according to regulations of Jewish law which sought to spare beasts needless suffering. The meat must then be soaked and salted to drain off the remaining blood. However, these are only a few of the laws of kashrus. There are many others, such as prohibitions against mixing meat and milk or eating both types of dishes at any one meal.

" 'Orthodox law,' he went on, 'also has many regulations about Jewish dress and ritual purity. . . .'

" 'Of course,' I broke in, and I proceeded to cite several examples. 'Since a Jew may not use a razor, he must wear a beard. Garments containing a mixture of linen and wool are forbidden. After marriage, a Jewish woman is expected to have her hair cut short and to wear a wig.'

" 'And don't forget the special ritual baths demanded by Orthodox law,' Rabbi Wise reminded me. 'They're to guarantee the ritual purity of Jewish men and women.'

" 'I see that the Pittsburgh Conference abolished all of these,' I remarked.

" 'Yes, indeed,' he assented. 'Such laws developed out of the needs of earlier periods of Jewish history, but we recognized that we have now outgrown these practices and that they need no longer be observed.'

"I returned to the written statement of the Pittsburgh Platform":

THE FIFTH PLANK

The Messianic Age

5.

WE look upon the modern period as the beginning of Israel's great age of truth, justice and peace for all mankind. We no longer expect to return to Palestine, nor do we seek to restore the Temple with its worship of sacrifices and burnt-offerings.

" 'This is actually a restatement of the principle adopted by the Philadelphia Rabbinical Conference of 1869,' I pointed out.

" 'That's right,' answered Rabbi Wise. 'In preparing a platform for Reform Judaism, we felt it necessary to emphasize this point. Our ideas of the Messianic Age were quite different from those of the Orthodox. We neither expect all Jews to return to Palestine, nor do we look forward to the restoration of ancient forms of worship in a rebuilt Temple. Furthermore, we no longer believe in the coming of any single individual known as the Messiah. Instead, we hold that a great Messianic Age will appear here on earth when all men accept Israel's teachings and practice truth, justice and peace. Israel's mission of spreading the teachings of God will hasten the coming of that day.' "

THE SIXTH PLANK
A Developing Judaism and Its Mission

6.

WE recognize that Judaism is constantly developing through adjustment to the needs of the times. At the same time, we must always preserve our connection with the Jewish past. We regard Christianity and Mohammedanism, both of which developed from Judaism, as assisting Israel in its mission of spreading Jewish teachings and hastening the coming of the Messianic Age.

" 'Here we present one of the most important principles of Reform Judaism,' Rabbi Wise declared.

" 'Do you mean the developing character of our religion?' I questioned.

" 'Precisely! The Orthodox teach that Judaism is the word of God and hence fixed for all times. But we insist that Judaism is a constantly changing, developing religion. We base our Reform point of view on the scientific discoveries of Zunz and other Jewish scholars who have proved that Judaism has continually modified its teachings and practices.'

" 'Yet, at the same time,' I pointed out, 'Reform represents no "break" with Jewish tradition. We trace back our own principles to those found in historic Jewish teachings.'

" 'Of course,' asserted Rabbi Wise. 'Reform is merely the continuing development of Judaism in the new and changed conditions of our modern world.' He paused a moment. 'Did you notice, too, that our Conference extended the hand of friendship to Christianity and Mohammedanism and urged their cooperation in promoting the Jewish principles of justice and righteousness among all men? In this way, our religion is aided in fulfilling its mission to the world.'

"I made no further comment and returned to the reading of the principles":

THE SEVENTH PLANK

Immortality of the Soul

7.

WE believe that the soul is immortal, and because it comes from God who demands righteousness, it finds its greatest happiness in the righteous deeds of its possessor. We reject all ideas of bodily resurrection of the dead and of everlasting punishment or reward in hell and heaven.

" 'Isn't this, too, based on one of the decisions of the Philadelphia Conference?' I questioned.

" 'Yes,' Rabbi Wise agreed. 'To be complete, our platform had to substitute belief in immortality of the soul in place of bodily resurrection. We hold that every individual's soul comes from God and is deathless like God Himself. After death the body gradually turns to dust, but the soul returns to God and lives on with Him forever.'

" 'In other words,' I said, 'Reform refused to accept the traditional belief that with the coming of the Messiah the dead would be bodily restored to life.'

" 'That's right,' he nodded, 'and we also eliminated all Orthodox ideas of heaven where the righteous are rewarded and hell where the wicked are punished.'

" 'On what grounds?' I sought to know.

" 'We considered these teachings foreign to our faith. They found their way into Judaism during the Persian period of our history, and, because they promised rewards for our suffering and punishment to our oppressors, they grew in popularity as our people underwent intense persecution. But even the rabbis of the Talmud objected to such beliefs as non-Jewish. At Pittsburgh we agreed that the reward of righteousness lies in the good deeds done here upon earth and the blessing they bring to others. Wickedness is punished by the sorrow it causes others and the sadness of the soul as it returns to God.'

"I now turned to the last article of the Pittsburgh Platform which deals with Social Justice":

THE EIGHTH PLANK

Social Justice

8.

IN keeping with the teachings of our Bible which demand fair treatment for poor and rich alike, and assistance for all who are oppressed, we consider it our duty to help overcome the evils of our world. We must help to end poverty in the midst of plenty, and eliminate the persecution and mistreatment of all races, peoples and religious groups.

" 'This final principle,' Rabbi Wise explained, 'establishes social justice as one of the most important ideals of Judaism. . . .'

" 'What exactly do you mean by the expression, "social justice"?' I wanted to know.

" 'Fair treatment for all peoples of society,' he answered. 'This principle is based on the teachings of our Prophets and is part of the mission of Israel in seeking to create a better world for mankind. Our religion commands all Jews to strive for the elimination of poverty, persecution, bad working conditions, and other evils found in modern society.'

"When Rabbi Wise had concluded I turned to him and said, 'From everything you've told me, the Pittsburgh Conference seems to have been very successful.'

" 'Yes, David. At last we've adopted a set of principles for Reform Judaism. . . .' "

*   *   *

"And that," declared Great-Grandfather, "was the conversation I had with Rabbi Wise."

"So That's the Pittsburgh Platform!" "So that's the Pittsburgh Platform!" Father spoke up. "I've heard our rabbi speak of it many times, but I never realized that it presented such a complete program."

"Remember, too," Great-Grandfather pointed out, "it represents some mighty important contributions to the progress of the Reform movement."

"What are they?" Mother asked, specifically.

"First of all," Great-Grandfather began, "the Pittsburgh Platform developed several new Reform ideas—ones not produced by any previous rabbinical meeting. For example, it established the principle that there was no conflict between the teachings of Judaism and the discoveries of science. It upheld the belief that Reform represented the most advanced stage of a continually developing Judaism. It proclaimed the ideal of social justice as a Jewish religious duty toward fulfilling the mission of Israel, and even invited the cooperation of other religions in bringing about the Messianic Age.

"Then, too, the Platform stated specifically which of the Orthodox ceremonies and practices Reform no longer accepted, for it abolished all laws which had regulated Jewish life in Palestine and those that prescribed special diet and dress.

"And finally," he concluded, "the Pittsburgh Platform unified American Reform Jewry with a single declaration of principles which served as an official statement of the movement for fifty-two years."

Betty started to figure. "Let's see," she counted aloud, "1885 plus 52 would bring us down to 1937." She turned to Great-Grandfather and asked, "What happened in that year?"

The Family Receives a Visitor. He was about to answer when the doorbell rang. Father excused himself to go to the door. The family heard Father say, "Why, come right in, Rabbi."

Mother peered into the hall. "It's Rabbi Cohen," she told the others.

Father ushered the rabbi of their temple into the living-room. "We're delighted to see you," Mother welcomed him as he entered. "Won't you sit down and join us?"

Great-Grandfather and Betty both greeted him. "I know you'll be interested in what we were discussing," Great-Grandfather told him.

"What were you discussing?" asked Rabbi Cohen.

"The Pittsburgh Platform," responded Betty. "I was just asking Great-Grandfather what happened to it in 1937."

"Well, now, suppose we let Rabbi Cohen tell us," suggested Great-Grandfather.

"Well," Rabbi Cohen started, "in 1937, the Reform rabbis adopted a new platform. . . ."

"But," Father objected, "if the Pittsburgh Platform satisfied the Reform movement for so long, what prompted the rabbis to create a new one?"

"Because," answered Rabbi Cohen, "our movement believes in meeting the needs of the times, and by 1937 Reform thinking in America had greatly changed. . . ."

"Changed?" Father was surprised. "But how?"

Betty, too, wondered at the rabbi's statement as she waited for his answer. . . .

QUESTIONS FOR DISCUSSION

1. How did the Philadelphia Rabbinical Conference represent an advance over European Reform?

2. What were the problems which the Pittsburgh Platform attempted to solve?

3. What were the most important contributions made by the Pittsburgh Conference to American Reform Judaism?

4. Why did Reform refuse to transfer the observance of the Jewish Sabbath to Sunday?

5. With what statements of the Pittsburgh Platform would Orthodox Jews agree and with which would they disagree?

6. How do present-day Reform beliefs and practices compare with those presented by the Pittsburgh Platform?

SUGGESTED ACTIVITIES

1. On the basis of your temple's practices draw up a new Reform platform. Then compare it with the one produced by the Pittsburgh Conference.

2. Create a news broadcast dealing with the creation of the Reform platform by the rabbis at Pittsburgh.

3. Conduct a debate on the subject: *"Resolved,* That the Pittsburgh Conference should have changed the Jewish Sabbath to Sunday."

ADDITIONAL READINGS FOR PUPILS

FEUER, LEON I. and AZRIEL EISENBERG, *Jewish Literature Since the Bible, II,* pp. 199-205.

GITTELSOHN, ROLAND B., *Modern Jewish Problems,* pp. 257 (N), 260 (V).

LEVINGER, LEE J., *A History of the Jews in the United States,* pp. 238-242.

SOLOFF, MORDECAI I., *How the Jewish People Lives Today,* pp. 176-187.

References for the Teacher

ELBOGEN, ISMAR, *A Century of Jewish Life,* pp. 343-345 (Pittsburgh Conference).

Jewish Encyclopedia, "Rabbinical Conferences," Vol. 4, pp. 214-215; "Kaufmann Kohler," Vol. 7, p. 533.

PHILIPSON, DAVID, *Central Conference of American Rabbis Yearbook,* "The Pittsburgh Rabbinical Conference," Vol. 45, pp. 190-206.

——, *The Reform Movement in Judaism,* pp. 353-357 (Philadelphia and Pittsburgh Conferences).

SCHWARTZMAN, SYLVAN D., *Reform Judaism in the Making,* Chap. 12, "Reform Produces the Pittsburgh Platform."

Universal Jewish Encyclopedia, "Rabbinical Conferences," Vol. 3, pp. 327-328; "Kaufmann Kohler," Vol. 6, pp. 428-430.

13. 1937 AND A NEW REFORM PLATFORM

But Why a New Platform? "I don't understand," declared Betty, shaking her head.

"What don't you understand?" Great-Grandfather asked her.

"Why Reform needed a new set of principles. No sooner do we get a platform for the Reform movement, than we change it."

"It didn't happen that quickly," Mother reminded Betty. "Remember, the Pittsburgh Platform appeared in 1885 and the new one wasn't adopted until 1937, fifty-two years later."

Father turned to Rabbi Cohen. "Rabbi," he suggested, "suppose you tell us why Reform had to adopt a new set of principles."

"I was just about to explain," said Rabbi Cohen. "There were at least five important reasons."

"Five!" exclaimed Betty. "I can't even think of one. . . ."

"Suppose," Great-Grandfather proposed, "we let Rabbi Cohen explain."

"By all means," agreed Father. "Please continue, Rabbi."

1. The End of the Reform Revolution. The family listened attentively as Rabbi Cohen started to speak.

"In the first place," he began, "we must understand that Reform Judaism started as a revolutionary movement in Jewish life—a revolt against an unchangeable Orthodoxy. Now, any revolution means violent, sudden change. In their enthusiasm for a cause, people frequently carry things to an extreme and destroy institutions and practices that have real value. The French Revolution did just that. In its early days it went to violent extremes in the name of 'liberty' in attacking religion and by executing many thousands of loyal Frenchmen who could not agree with every revolutionary measure."

Betty spoke up. "I suppose, then, that the early Reform movement went to extremes, too."

"Unfortunately, yes," was Rabbi Cohen's reply. "Some of the early leaders, particularly in America, were radical Reformers. In their revolt against Orthodox Judaism, they proceeded to do away with certain ceremonies which could have been of great religious inspiration to our people. Under their direction, the movement also ignored important Jewish influences, such as religious practice in the home, which were essential to the survival of our religion.

"But it was among some of their lay followers that Reform was carried to the greatest extremes," Rabbi Cohen explained, and he offered several illustrations. "To some, Reform Judaism meant a complete break with all of Jewish tradition. When the Pittsburgh Platform declared that the Talmud was no longer binding in matters of dress, diet and ceremonies, some immediately took the attitude that the whole Talmud was worthless. Others objected to certain Jewish practices simply because they were also observed by the Orthodox. Some even regarded Reform as sanctioning every change that suited personal convenience."

"This certainly was a far cry from the Reform of an Isaac Mayer Wise," Great-Grandfather remarked. "His purpose was to produce a Reform that would strengthen the Judaism of the modern Jew, not weaken it."

"Naturally," Rabbi Cohen agreed, "the more moderate Reformers like Wise were alarmed. But they hoped that as time passed such Reform radicalism would grow less extreme. They recalled how the early violence of the French Revolution had eventually given way to orderly democratic government."

"And were they right?" Mother questioned.

"Yes," replied the rabbi. "As the years passed and the movement grew in numbers and became better organized, the early radicalism began to subside. But in the process the Pittsburgh Platform became more and more unsuitable."

"Why?" Father wanted to know.

"Mainly because it was a product of Reform's revolutionary period. The Pittsburgh Platform was as much a statement of opposition to Orthodox belief as it was a declaration of Reform's teachings. In the fifty-two years between the Pittsburgh Conference and 1937, new generations of more moderate Reform leaders appeared, and they sought a set of principles that would be representative of the later developments of the movement."

"Now I begin to understand," said Mother. "The Pittsburgh Platform endorsed extreme Reform while the movement was now advocating a moderate Reform."

"That's it exactly," declared Rabbi Cohen.

2. Changes in the Composition of American Jewry. "Secondly," Rabbi

Cohen continued, "Reform had need of a new platform because of the changes that had taken place in the American Jewish community. The composition of American Jewry was far different in 1937 from what it had been in the years before 1885."

"Different?" questioned Betty. "In what way?"

"In 1880, for instance, there were about 300,000 Jews in the whole United States. Most of them had come from Germany and many belonged to Reform congregations. In fact, some Reform leaders were then predicting that all American Jews would soon become Reform. At the time, such statements appeared justified because the number of Orthodox Jews was dwindling while Reform membership was rapidly expanding. But something happened to change the entire picture."

"What was that?" Mother inquired.

"In 1881," Rabbi Cohen responded, "an official of the Russian government announced that one-third of Russian Jewry would be compelled to accept Christianity, another third would be starved to death, and the last third driven from the country. Physical attacks against the Jews now became frequent; many were killed and much property destroyed. The Russian government then expelled those living in western Russia and crowded all six million Russian Jews into the small section called 'The Pale of Jewish Settlement.' Unable to bear their suffering any longer, thousands began to flee the country and they came principally to the United States. Between 1881 and 1910 over a million Russian Jews entered the country; during the same period 350,000 more came from other sections of eastern Europe. All told, between the years of 1880 and 1937, about two million immigrated to America."

"I don't see how this affected the Reform movement," said Betty.

"Remember," Rabbi Cohen explained, "practically all of these new immigrants were strictly Orthodox in their religious beliefs. Before coming to America, few of them had ever enjoyed freedom; consequently, they had little contact with Reform Judaism. The result was that Reform in the United States now found itself a small minority in the midst of several million Orthodox Jews."

"But weren't these newcomers attracted to the movement?" Father wanted to know.

"Not at first," replied Rabbi Cohen. "Reform seemed so strange to them that they would have nothing to do with it. Only gradually, as they and their children grew accustomed to American ways, did many of them begin to realize the impossibility of maintaining their former type of Judaism. Like the early Reformers, they, too, sought modernization of Orthodox services and customs, but the majority still regarded Reform as too radical a change."

"Didn't any become Reform?" Betty wondered.

"Certainly. Quite a few did join Reform congregations and become active members," Rabbi Cohen asserted, "and they brought with them into the movement a new appreciation for traditional ceremonies. They pointed out that many of these rituals, such as the chanting of the kiddush and the blowing of the shofor, had real beauty and meaning for the modern Jew and insisted that they would add much to the religious spirit of the movement."

"And how did the congregations respond to this?" asked Mother.

"The growing numbers of these new members and the appeal of their argument prompted some Reform temples to introduce more ceremonies into the worship. In addition, new rituals were also created for special religious occasions. Gradually, these congregations began to attract even greater numbers of new members."

"But other Reform Jews," Rabbi Cohen disclosed, "questioned some of these newly-introduced practices. 'Were they acceptable to the movement?' they asked, and they pointed to the Pittsburgh Platform with its statement that only meaningful ceremonies were to be considered binding upon the Reform Jew."

"I can certainly see why a new platform would be needed," Father commented. "In view of the rapidly changing situation, the movement required some new official statement on the matter of ceremonials."

"Correct!" Rabbi Cohen said emphatically. "Some Reform leaders were insisting that a new platform was necessary in order to win the masses of American Jews to Reform, and many more were agreed that the needs of the times called for revisions in the Pittsburgh principles."

3. The Rise of Anti-Semitism. "What was the third development that influenced Reform?" Great-Grandfather asked Rabbi Cohen.

"The rise of anti-Semitism," was his reply. "Following World War I and its hardships, Europe witnessed an alarming growth of organized anti-Jewish movements. In Germany, the Nazi party came into being. Throughout Poland, Rumania, Hungary and other European lands, violent attacks against the Jews became common. When, in 1933, Adolf Hitler took over control of Germany, anti-Semitism became the law of the country and the mass-murder of German Jewry quickly followed. Strong anti-Semitic Fascist parties now existed in practically every European country."

"But that was Europe," Betty objected.

"America, too," the rabbi hastened to explain, "was experiencing a rising tide of anti-Semitism. First came the Ku Klux Klan and other 'hate' organizations spreading prejudice in all sections of our country and greatly influencing public opinion against the Jews. From 1920 to 1927, for example, even one of America's leading automobile manufacturers carried on a public campaign against the Jews in his weekly newspaper.

"After a while, the more active demonstrations of anti-Semitism waned, only to be replaced by other discriminations against our people. Jews began to find difficulty in obtaining certain types of employment. Well-known colleges and universities placed limitations upon the number of Jewish students they would admit. Many hotels, summer resorts and residential areas refused to accept Jews. And, by 1937, Nazi agents in this country were already at work circulating their German anti-Semitism."

"How did the American Jews react to all of this?" Mother inquired of the rabbi.

"It made most of them uneasy about the future," he answered. "While serious trouble never arose in this country, our people felt themselves threatened by the continued anti-Semitism and they reacted as Jews did in former periods of their history. They turned toward their religion and their fellow Jews for comfort and strength. Many Reform Jews now became conscious of the extremes to which the movement had been carried during its revolutionary period. They began to demand a closer association of Reform with world Israel and the restoration of some of the Jewish observances that had been eliminated. They also recommended more intensive Jewish education for their children, greater religious practice in their homes, more Hebrew in worship, and other measures."

"And this served as another argument for changing the Pittsburgh Platform, didn't it?" Betty said.

"Yes," Rabbi Cohen admitted. "For one thing, Reform leaders objected to its statement that the modern world was the beginning of Israel's great Messianic Age of truth, justice, and peace. 'Was this still true,' they questioned, 'in view of the growing hatred of the Jews?' Then again, they saw the need of some new declaration of principles that would emphasize the importance of Jewish observance and education. The Pittsburgh Platform, they concluded, did not fully express the more recent Jewish experiences and Reform requirements."

4. The Growth of Zionism. "Didn't the growth of Zionism, too, lead to a demand for a new Reform platform?" Great-Grandfather suggested.

"Yes," answered Rabbi Cohen, "that was certainly another powerful factor."

"You realize, of course," Great-Grandfather pointed out to the others, "that in 1885, when the Pittsburgh Platform was adopted, there wasn't any organized Zionist movement. True, there were some 'Lovers of Zion' societies in existence during this period, but the effort to rebuild a Jewish State didn't become a definite reality until 1897 when the first Zionist Congress met in Basle, Switzerland, and declared itself in favor of establishing a Jewish Homeland in Palestine."

"Precisely," agreed Rabbi Cohen. "It was Theodor Herzl, a distinguished Viennese journalist, who founded modern Zionism. He had been sent by his newspaper to report on the Dreyfus trial in France."

"Great-Grandfather told us a good deal about the Dreyfus Affair," Betty informed him. "Captain Alfred Dreyfus was the officer on the French General Staff who, in 1894, was accused of selling military secrets to the Germans. He was declared guilty of treason and sent to prison, although he was later proved innocent. It seems, too, that certain powerful Frenchmen used the fact that Dreyfus was a Jew to try to overthrow the French republic. They told the French people that, just like Dreyfus, none of the Jews could be trusted. Therefore, any democratic government which promoted Jews to high rank in the army was dangerous to France. But, as we know, those who said such things wanted to destroy democracy only in order to rule the country themselves."

"That's absolutely right, Betty,"

the rabbi complimented her, "and Theodor Herzl found himself in the midst of that struggle. He listened to the cries of 'down with the Jews!' that echoed throughout France and was shocked by the violent anti-Semitism that existed in so liberal a land. He came to the conclusion that the only hope for the Jewish people was to have a state of their own, and he was moved to write the book, *The Jewish State*, which attracted wide attention and led to the formation of the World Zionist Organization."

"Isn't it true," Mother asked, "that many of the early Reform leaders opposed Zionism?"

"Yes," answered Great-Grandfather, "but there were also some who played a prominent role in the development of the Zionist movement. In fact, Rabbi Bernhard Felsenthal helped form the first Zionist society in the United States, and Rabbi Stephen S. Wise, Dr. Gustav Gottheil and his son, Professor Richard Gottheil, organized the Federation of American Zionists in 1898."

"As time passed," added Rabbi Cohen, "more and more Reform rabbis became identified with the Zionist cause, and some were its greatest leaders. By 1937, a considerable majority of Reform rabbis supported the movement. The Zionist anthem, 'Hatikvo,' already appeared in the *Union Hymnal* and there was a growing demand for special prayers supporting the upbuilding of Palestine in the *Union Prayerbook*."

"How was it that the idea of Zionism spread so rapidly?" asked Father.

"The happenings of the times," he responded, "were chiefly responsible. Beginning with the pogroms in Russia and the spread of violent anti-Semitism in other European lands, the position of many European Jews grew less and less secure. Some practical solution to their plight became a growing necessity. A ready answer appeared in the movement which sought to establish a Jewish Homeland in Palestine. There, it was maintained, those people who found life no longer bearable in various European countries could start life anew.

"Meanwhile, the Zionist cause received special encouragement in 1917 when the British government issued the Balfour Declaration in which it officially promised to assist the Jewish people in rebuilding Palestine as a Jewish Homeland. This pledge was repeated by the League of Nations in 1922 when it appointed Great Britain as guardian over Palestine.

"The movement continued to grow slowly. Many were attracted to Zionism out of admiration for the remarkable accomplishments of the Palestinian Jews. In spite of the fact that the country had been so badly neglected for centuries, early Jewish settlers managed to establish several thriving colonies. Gradually, the pioneering work of Jews who were now entering Palestine in ever-increasing numbers attracted world-wide attention. They drained the swamps, eliminated the serious diseases of the area, built hundreds of farm colonies, developed irrigation and electric power, constructed modern cities, established an excellent school system and the Hebrew University, and transformed Hebrew into the living language of the land.

"Then, in 1933 disaster struck an important section of European Jewry when Adolf Hitler seized control of Germany and his Nazi party commenced its brutal attacks against the Jews. Escaping the country as best they could, thousands of German refugees poured into Palestine. By 1937, as the terrible persecutions spread to other lands, nearly 400,000 Jews had entered Palestine, and many more were preparing to come.

"Naturally, Jews all over the world felt it their duty to assist their European brethren. They raised huge sums of money to carry on relief work and to support the building of the Jewish Homeland. Many more thousands of American Jews joined the official Zionist movement, and quite a few came from the ranks of Reform."

"But, at the same time, there were also a number of Reform Jews who objected to Zionism," Great-Grandfather observed.

"That's true," Rabbi Cohen admitted. "Some Reform Jews did not believe that our people should have a state of their own, and they pointed to the fifth principle of the Pittsburgh Platform to prove that Reform was opposed to a 'return to Zion.'

"However, those who were sympathetic to Zionism argued that the early Reform rabbis had objected to the Orthodox idea of a Messianic 'return of all Jews from exile to Palestine' and not to the Zionist movement of the twentieth century. Actually, the Pittsburgh Platform had appeared before the rise of the political Zionist movement and those who wrote it could not foresee the modern creation of a Jewish Homeland in Palestine. Reform Judaism, they insisted, must now take into account the new situation of world and American Jewry."

"And that became still another reason for demanding a new Reform platform," Great-Grandfather summarized.

5. Dissatisfaction with Reform's Progress. "Finally," Rabbi Cohen disclosed, "there were some Reform leaders who were dissatisfied with the movement's lagging progress in America. They were disturbed by the negligible increase in membership during the early 1930's and contended that Reform, which had been created to satisfy the religious needs of emancipated Jews, was failing to attract most American Jews to the movement.

"They claimed that Reform had other shortcomings. They maintained that the attachments of some members to Judaism and the Jewish people were beginning to weaken. A number of Reform Jews came to temple services only during the High Holydays; some never attended the synagogue. Others had come to regard their Reform Judaism as simply a series of beliefs requiring little or no religious practice, and still others felt little kinship with world Jewry."

"Was the Pittsburgh Platform held responsible for this, too?" Father asked.

"To some degree, yes," Rabbi Cohen asserted. "Reform rabbis criticized the Pittsburgh Platform for stressing the beliefs of Reform without, at the same time, emphasizing the religious obligations of Reform Jews. Experience had shown that a new emphasis had to be placed upon home, synagogue and Jewish community responsibilities in order to preserve the strong attachment of Reform members to Judaism and their fellow Jews."

"And they wanted this included in the new Reform principles?" questioned Betty.

"Right!"

Reform Gets a New Platform. "So these are the five main reasons for the new Reform platform," Mother commented.

"And don't forget," Great-Grandfather reminded them, "according to its own teachings, Reform not only had the right but also the duty to change in order to meet the new needs of the times."

"That was the argument many rabbis used in urging the preparation of a new set of principles," Rabbi Cohen asserted. "Finally, in 1937, after several years of discussion, the Central Conference of American Rabbis, meeting in Columbus, Ohio, adopted 'The Guiding Principles of Reform Judaism.'"

"What are some of its main points?" Father asked.

"It consists of three major sections —first, the central beliefs of Reform; second, its ethical teachings; and third, the religious duties of Reform members. . . ."

"Aha!" exclaimed Betty, "I see that they did include statements on Reform practice."

"I happen to have with me some copies of a digest of the 'Guiding Principles,'" said the rabbi, and reaching into his pocket, he pulled out several printed sheets. He distributed one to each member of the family.

"As you read it," he suggested, "see how it compares with the Pittsburgh Platform. Try to decide where it agrees with the 1885 statement and how it differs."

The room grew quiet as the family began to look over the Digest of the 1937 Principles. This is what they read:

A DIGEST

"The Guiding Principles of Reform Judaism"

I. Judaism and Its Foundations

1. Nature of Judaism. Judaism, which grew out of the experiences of the Jewish people, looks forward to the perfection of all mankind. Reform accepts the principle of growth and change in religion, and sees no conflict between its teachings and the discoveries of science.

2. God. The heart of Judaism and its most important contribution to religion is its belief in the one living God who rules the world. He is both the Creator of the universe and our merciful Father.

3. Man. All men possess an immortal soul and are the children of the one God. As such, man must seek to overcome evil and do only that which is good.

4. *Torah.* The Bible, Talmud and other great Jewish works remain the source of our religion. Although the conditions of modern life have made certain of their laws no longer binding, each age should apply their teachings to the needs of the Jewish people.

5. *Israel.* Living in all parts of the world, the Jewish people are bound together by ties of common history and religion. While we continue to recognize Jews who are not religious as members of the Jewish people, we look upon religion as Israel's greatest uniting force. The non-Jew who accepts Judaism is considered a complete member of the Jewish community.

Wherever our people have been granted their freedom, they have become loyal citizens. At the same time, all Jews have a duty to help build the Jewish Homeland in Palestine for the sake of those who are oppressed and as a center of Jewish learning and religion.

Israel's mission is to spread God's teachings throughout the world so that, in cooperation with all peoples, a Messianic Age of justice, truth and peace shall be established here upon earth.

II. Ethics

6. *Ethics and Religion.* Righteousness and love of our fellow man are essential teachings of our religion. Therefore, Judaism insists upon freedom and justice for all men of every race, religion and class, and regards these aims as the main purpose for which governments exist.

7. *Social Justice.* Judaism strives for a just society in which poverty, tyranny, slavery, and hatred will no longer exist. For all who work, we urge fair wages and proper working conditions, and we uphold the right of all men to protection in old age, sickness and unemployment.

8. *Peace.* Judaism has always proclaimed the ideal of a peaceful world founded upon justice. To this end, we seek the creation of strong international organization to prevent further war.

III. Religious Practice

9. *The Religious Life.* Our religion requires that its followers participate fully in Jewish life through the maintenance of a Jewish home, the synagogue, school, and other institutions that promote the welfare of the Jewish people.

The Jewish home must be founded

upon righteousness and religious practice.

The synagogue, which is the oldest and most important institution in Jewish life, must be properly supported.

A thorough Jewish education for each generation of our people is most essential.

Judaism also demands regular prayer both at home and in the synagogue, and the preservation of the Sabbath, Festivals and Holydays. It calls for the reintroduction and development of inspiring customs, symbols and ceremonies, the creation of religious art and music, and the use of Hebrew together with English in religious worship and religious instruction.

The New Principles and the Pittsburgh Platform. "I find that a good many teachings of the Pittsburgh Platform were retained," remarked Father as the family finished reading the "Guiding Principles."

"Yes, there were quite a few," Mother stated, and she proceeded to list several. "The Jewish idea of God as Israel's most important contribution, the essential agreement between Judaism and science, the right of Judaism to change to meet new conditions. . . ."

"And don't forget the mission of Israel, the Messianic Age of righteousness and peace, and the principle of social justice," Betty added.

"In spite of its shortcomings," commented Great-Grandfather, "you can see that the Pittsburgh Platform was an important Reform achievement."

"Nevertheless," Mother pointed out to him, "did you notice the more moderate tone of the new platform? It makes no attack on Orthodox beliefs but simply states the Reform principles."

"How many changes did you find in the 1937 platform, Betty?" Rabbi Cohen asked.

"At least half a dozen," she replied and she began to call them out. "Reform Jews should assist in the rebuilding of Palestine, strengthen the Jewish home, synagogue and other Jewish institutions, provide young people with a more thorough Jewish education. . . ." She couldn't remember any more.

Mother came to her rescue. "Wider use of Hebrew in worship and religious education," she added, "and the inclusion of more ceremonies in services. . . ."

"Don't forget the greater emphasis upon regular prayer both at home and in the synagogue," Great-Grandfather called out.

"These certainly prove that Reform was in need of a new platform," asserted Father.

"And they also show," Mother ob-

A COMPARISON OF THE PITTSBURGH PLATFORM
AND THE GUIDING PRINCIPLES

	The Pittsburgh Platform—1885	The Guiding Principles—1937
JUDAISM'S GOD-IDEA	Judaism presents the highest idea of God	Judaism's God-idea is central in the Jewish faith and its most important contribution to religion
RESURRECTION AND IMMORTALITY	Reform rejects all belief in heavenly rewards and punishments in hell, as well as bodily resurrection. Instead, Reform believes only in the immortality of the soul	Man possesses an immortal soul
MESSIANIC BELIEF	Reform no longer expects the coming of a personal Messiah. Rather, it regards the present time as the approach of Israel's Messianic Age of truth, justice and peace	In cooperation with all peoples, Israel hopes to establish a Messianic Age of justice, truth and peace upon earth
PALESTINE	A return of the Jews to Palestine is *not* sought	All Jews are obliged to aid in the upbuilding of Palestine as the Jewish Homeland
THE JEWISH PEOPLE	Jews are no longer a nation but a religious community	Jews are bound together by their common history and religion. Even non-religious Jews remain members of the Jewish people
THE MISSION OF ISRAEL	Israel welcomes the aid of other faiths in helping it fulfill its Mission of spreading the teachings of the one God	Israel's mission is to spread the knowledge of God and cooperate with all men in bringing about the Messianic Age
SOCIAL JUSTICE	It is the duty of the Jew to help solve the issues of social justice	Judaism strives for a just society in which poverty, tyranny, slavery and hatred are abolished
WORLD PEACE		Judaism seeks a peaceful world founded on justice and strives for strong international organization to prevent war
RELIGIOUS PRACTICE	Only ceremonies in keeping with modern life are acceptable. Laws regulating diet, dress, and ritual purity are abolished	Jews are expected to participate fully in the Jewish life of the home, synagogue, school and other institutions. Judaism requires prayer, observance of the Sabbath and holidays, symbols and ceremonies, and the use of Hebrew
JEWISH TRADITION	Judaism is a developing religion. It must preserve its connection with the past but the Bible and Talmud as a whole are no longer binding	Reform recognizes that Judaism is a developing religion. The Written and Oral Law are the source of Judaism but must be adapted to the needs of each generation
JUDAISM AND SCIENCE	Judaism and science are not in conflict. Biblical stories of miracles and other incidents are legends of earlier times	The discoveries of modern science do not conflict with the essential teachings of Judaism

served, "how the movement was influenced by the five changes that had taken place since the days of the Pittsburgh Platform."

Betty Calls for Another Chart. For a moment everyone was quiet. Then as Betty's eyes fell upon Great-Grandfather's chart of the decisions of European Reform, she spoke up. "Rabbi Cohen," she asked, "did Reform in America ever settle all of the religious problems it failed to solve in Europe?"

"What sort of problems are you referring to, Betty?" he wanted to know.

"Questions like Jewish marriage and divorce laws, mourning customs, and the religious rights of Jewish women," she explained.

"How do you know about such things?" the rabbi asked in complete surprise.

"Oh," she said, "we've talked a good bit about them. In fact, we even have Great-Grandfather's chart of European Reform," and with that she handed him the chart.

He examined it carefully. "Excellent," he complimented Great-Grandfather and then he added, "but you know, of course, that you haven't brought it up to date. . . ."

"That's why I asked the question," Betty quickly replied. "Isn't it time that we charted American Reform practices, too?"

"Surely, Betty," agreed the rabbi. "Let's go right to work on it. . . ."

QUESTIONS FOR DISCUSSION

1. What were the changes in Jewish life after 1885 that led to the demand for a new Reform platform?
2. Why was the Pittsburgh Platform considered inadequate for the needs of the Reform movement in the middle 1930's?
3. How did the Guiding Principles attempt to meet the new needs of the Reform Jew?
4. In what respects do the Pittsburgh Platform and the Guiding Principles agree and disagree?
5. What changes have taken place in Reform's official attitude toward Palestine?
6. How is the new Reform platform reflected in the practices of your temple today?

SUGGESTED ACTIVITIES

1. Prepare a chart showing the major differences between the Reform platforms of 1885 and 1937.
2. Create a series of posters which illustrate the changes that took place in American and world Jewish life after 1885.
3. Produce a dramatic sketch telling of (a) the immigration of the east European Jew to America, (b) the rise of the Zionist movement, or (c) the growth of anti-Semitism in the post-World War I period.

ADDITIONAL READINGS FOR PUPILS

FEUER, LEON I. and AZRIEL EISENBERG, *Jewish Literature Since the Bible, II,* pp. 263-268.

GITTELSOHN, ROLAND B., *Modern Jewish Problems,* pp. 162 (F), 234-235 (C), 252 (A), 257-258 (P), 258 (R), 259 (S and T).

GOLUB, JACOB S. and ALAN S. GREEN, *A Short History of the Jews, III,* pp. 28-29, 32-38, 52-53, 66-79, 97-103.

KALISHER, BETTY, *Watchmen of the Night,* pp. 198-205.

LEVINGER, LEE J., *A History of the Jews in the United States,* pages 9-16, 261-280, 536-539, 541-546, 556-557.

LURIE, ROSE G., *The Great March, II,* pp. 202-216.

SOLOFF, MORDECAI I., *How the Jewish People Lives Today,* pp. 253-281, 293-306.

References for the Teacher

Central Conference of American Rabbis Yearbook, Vol. 47, pp. 94-114 (adoption of the Guiding Principles).

ELBOGEN, ISMAR, *A Century of Jewish Life,* Book 4, Chap. 3, "The Jews of America at the Beginning of the Twentieth Century"; Book 5, Chap. 5, "The Jewish National Home in Palestine"; Chap. 6, "Hitler's Total War against the Jews."

MARCUS, JACOB R., *The Rise and Destiny of the German Jew,* Chap. 4, "Adolf Hitler and Nazi Anti-Semitism."

MASSERMAN, PAUL and MAX BAKER, *The Jews Come to America,* Chap. 12, "The Russian Jew in America"; Chap. 16, "Zionism in America."

SACHAR, ABRAM L., *A History of the Jews,* pp. 380-383, 394-396 (Zionism).

SCHWARTZMAN, SYLVAN D., *Reform Judaism in the Making,* Chap. 13, "1885–1935 — A Half-Century of Change"; Chap. 14, "Reform's Present Principles."

Universal Jewish Encyclopedia, "Judaism in America (Reform Judaism)," Vol. 6, pp. 242-243.

14. BETTY CHARTS REFORM'S PROGRESS

Let's Bring Reform Up to Date!
"I'm all ready," Betty called out to Rabbi Cohen as she brought out a pencil and pad. "And here is the chart of European Reform Judaism," she said, holding it up.

"Good," Rabbi Cohen said enthusiastically. "We'll need that if we are to see how Reform in America met the various problems that the European Reformers discussed."

"Aren't there also some questions which the European conferences didn't take up?" asked Mother.

"Yes," Rabbi Cohen replied, "there are several—the wearing of hats at services is one. We'll also include them," he assured her, "as we record the progress of American Reform."

"What type of chart will we need?" questioned Betty.

"Let's see," he considered. "We'll want five columns," he came to the conclusion. "One for the problem itself, another for Orthodox practice, a third to explain why reforms were

needed, a column for the decisions of European Reform, and the final one for modern American Reform practice."

"Righto!" Betty agreed as she ruled the lines and entered the proper headings. "Now let's bring Reform Judaism up to date!"

The Use of Hebrew in the Service.
"Suppose we start with the question of Hebrew in worship," suggested the rabbi. "According to the Orthodox practice, as you remember, the entire service is always conducted in Hebrew. . . ."

"And the difficulty," Great-Grandfather hastened to point out, "is that many Jews no longer understand Hebrew well enough to follow and enjoy the service."

"Exactly," Rabbi Cohen said, and he then turned to Betty. "Suppose you tell us the conclusions European Reform reached."

She glanced over the sheet before her. "The leaders agreed that only part of the service should be read in Hebrew," was her answer. "The rest could be conducted in whatever language the people understood."

"Actually," Rabbi Cohen asserted, "that is also present-day American Reform practice. But please remember that the 1937 Guiding Principles reemphasized the necessity for some Hebrew in temple worship."

Betty proceeded to fill in the first chart.

Problem	Orthodox Practice	Why Reforms Were Needed	European Reform	American Reform
USE OF HEBREW IN WORSHIP	All-Hebrew service	Many no longer enjoyed or understood the all-Hebrew service	Worship may be conducted partly in Hebrew and partly in the language of the land	Both Hebrew and English should be used in the service

Music in Religious Services. The next question Rabbi Cohen raised was that of music in the service. "Because of several objections by Jewish tradition," he explained, "the Orthodox forbid the use of instrumental music in the synagogue. Moreover, playing the organ on the Sabbath is regarded as a violation of the day's rest. Actually, then, only the cantor and an all-male choir are permitted to render the music of the service. There can be no mixed choir because of the prohibition against men and women sitting together."

Betty then reported the progress of European Reform. "The rabbis of Europe," she stated, "gave their approval to the use of the organ and other instrumental music, and the mixed choir in synagogue worship."

"Once again," Rabbi Cohen pointed out, "European Reform set the pattern for the movement in the United States. At temple, as you know, we use both the organ and mixed choir, and occasionally we introduce other instruments that add beauty to the service, such as the violin during Confirmation."

Betty jotted down this information for her second chart.

Problem	Orthodox Practice	Why Reforms Were Needed	European Reform	American Reform
MUSIC IN THE SERVICE	Instrumental music and mixed choir prohibited Only cantor and male choir permitted	Many desired more inspiring music in worship	Instrumental music and mixed choir permitted in services	Instrumental music and mixed choir permitted in services

Praying with Covered Heads. "We now come to one of those problems that the European leaders never discussed," Rabbi Cohen told Mother. "I refer to the matter of praying with covered heads."

"You're right," Betty remarked. "There isn't a word about it on the chart of European Reform."

"We know that in Orthodox Judaism," Father commented, "every man is required to wear some head-covering whenever he enters the synagogue or participates in a Jewish service."

"Interestingly enough," Rabbi Cohen disclosed, "the first congregation to eliminate the wearing of a head-covering was one right here in the United States—the Charleston Reform Society—which, in 1824, began conducting services without hats. In Europe it commenced in 1845 with the Berlin Reform Society and to date only a few congregations abroad have adopted the prac-

tice. In the United States, of course, the usual Reform custom today is to pray without hats."

"After all," Great-Grandfather pointed out, "there is no definite Talmudic law that demands the wearing of hats at religious services. The custom originated during periods of Jewish settlement in oriental lands where a head-covering was a mark of respect, but in the Western world one shows respect, as to a lady or the flag, by taking off his hat."

"Have we in the United States adopted any official decision on the question?" Father inquired.

"No," answered the rabbi, "but it is understood that Reform permits members to pray either with or without hats. Most Reform congregations have abolished the covering of the head, but there are still some which require their members or rabbis to wear hats."

In a few moments, Betty had finished this chart.

Problem	Orthodox Practice	Why Reforms Were Needed	European Reform	American Reform
PRAYING WITH COVERED HEADS	Men must wear a head-covering in the synagogue and whenever engaged in prayer	This was contrary to the practice of showing respect in the Western world	No decision was reached Several temples abolished head-coverings	Worship with or without head-coverings permitted General Reform practice is to pray bare-headed

The Religious Rights of Women. "I'm especially interested in the mat-

ter of women's religious rights," Mother informed Rabbi Cohen. "I

A member of the National Federation of Temple Sisterhoods conducts an Institute on Judaism for leaders of Christian church women's groups.

recall that according to Orthodox law Jewish women may not sit with men at services nor be counted toward a minyon. Moreover, they are not permitted to serve as witnesses in any ritual matter or conduct any portion of the service. . . ."

"European Reform made only one change," Betty promptly called out. "The Augsburg Synod agreed that women might act as full witnesses in all Jewish ritual matters."

"And what conclusions," Mother wanted to know, "have American Reform leaders reached?"

"We accept the principle of complete religious equality for Jewish women," the rabbi asserted.

"When was this adopted?" Mother asked.

"It came about gradually," the rabbi explained. "In 1852, for exam-

ple, at the dedication of the Bene Israel Synagogue in Cincinnati, women were given the right to sing in the choir. Later, Reform temples permitted men and women to sit together, and, at the 1891 convention of the Union of American Hebrew Congregations, a woman served as a congregational delegate."

"In all Reform temples today, of course," Father remarked, "men and women sit together, women are counted toward the minyon, and on special occasions, they even conduct the service."

"Not only that," Rabbi Cohen added, "but through their temple Sisterhoods, Reform women are extremely active in religious affairs. In fact, many are even full members of congregational boards."

Betty's chart was now complete.

Problem	Orthodox Practice	Why Reforms Were Needed	European Reform	American Reform
RELIGIOUS RIGHTS OF WOMEN	Separate synagogue section for women Women not included in minyon Women prohibited from conducting the worship or serving as witnesses in ritual matters	The inequality of women was contrary to both Judaism's belief in complete democracy and the Western world's greater religious privileges for women	Equality was recommended but no official action was taken Women permitted to serve as witnesses in ritual matters	Women granted complete equality They may sit with the men, conduct the service, and be counted toward a minyon

Observance of the Sabbath. "One of the most difficult problems that faced Reform was that of Sabbath observance," Rabbi Cohen stated. "Unfortunately, modern conditions make it necessary for large numbers of Jews to attend to their jobs or businesses on the Sabbath. This, of course, conflicts with Orthodox Sabbath services at sundown on Friday night and during Saturday morning. Most Jews find it practically impossible to attend either service, but for those who can, the great distances from home to synagogue make riding on the Sabbath a necessity. However, Orthodox law does not permit this."

Betty had been examining the chart of European Reform. "I see that the Reform rabbis of Europe approved of riding on the Sabbath in order to attend services," she announced.

"What's more," Great-Grandfather revealed, "as early as 1845, the Frankfort Reform Society recommended the conducting of special Sunday worship, and in the very same year, the Berlin Reform Society actually held such services."

"That's quite true," Rabbi Cohen admitted, "but these were exceptions to the general practice of European Reform. In America, however, the problem was more widely met. . . ."

"In what way?" Father wanted to know.

"As early as 1866," the rabbi responded, "Rabbi Isaac Mayer Wise introduced the late Friday evening service. This made it possible for whole families to attend the synagogue together on the Sabbath eve, and the idea was soon adopted by many congregations. Another proposal, introduced by a Baltimore Reform society in 1854, was a Sunday morning service in addition to regular Saturday worship. This, too, was tried in other temples."

"I recall that the more moderate Reform rabbis objected to services on Sunday," Father reminded the rabbi.

"In spite of that," he replied, "the Pittsburgh Conference of 1885 agreed that there was no Jewish law which prohibited the holding of such services. Furthermore, in 1902, while the Central Conference of American Rabbis insisted upon the preservation of Saturday as the Sabbath, it prepared a ritual for week-day services for those congregations that conducted Sunday worship. In 1904, the Conference again endorsed its 1902 resolution."

"Today, of course, most American Reform congregations hold late Friday evening services, beginning around eight o'clock, as well as Saturday morning worship," Great-Grandfather observed.

"Some, not many, also conduct a Sunday morning service," the rabbi added. "By arranging worship at these more convenient times," he explained, "American Reform Judaism both preserved the Saturday Sabbath and made it possible for modern Jews to attend the synagogue."

This was Betty's chart on the Sabbath question:

Problem	Orthodox Practice	Why Reforms Were Needed	European Reform	American Reform
OBSERV-ANCE OF THE SABBATH	Friday evening services held at sundown Riding to the synagogue prohibited	Modern working conditions prevented Sabbath synagogue attendance Distances from the synagogue made riding necessary	Riding to synagogue on the Sabbath permitted Sunday morning services introduced in addition to Sabbath worship	Riding to synagogue on the Sabbath permitted Adoption of late Friday evening and Sunday morning services in addition to regular Saturday worship

Extra Days of Holidays. "We come next to the issue of extra days in Jewish holiday observance. Here," Rabbi Cohen announced, "American Reform went even one step further than the movement in Europe."

"European Reform," Betty noted as she checked through the chart,

"decided that, with the exception of Rosh Ha-shono, there was no longer any reason for continuing the observance of extra days. They considered the Jewish calendar so well established that there could be no error in determining the proper dates for the celebration of the holidays."

"Why did they make an exception in the case of Rosh Ha-shono?" Father questioned.

It was Great-Grandfather who answered. "Because," he explained, "even in Palestine where the extra days had not been added, Rosh Ha-shono was celebrated for two days instead of one."

"American Reform maintains that Rosh Ha-shono, too, should be commemorated for only one day," Rabbi Cohen declared. "Thus we have adopted the number of days for holiday observance as commanded by the words of the Bible. Passover, for instance, is celebrated for seven days instead of eight; Shovuos is observed for one day instead of two, and so on."

This is the way Betty's chart appeared:

Problem	Orthodox Practice	Why Reforms Were Needed	European Reform	American Reform
EXTRA DAYS OF HOLIDAYS	Outside of Palestine an extra day of Jewish holidays was observed because of early difficulty in establishing correct dates	Creation of a permanent calendar made it unnecessary to add extra days to the holidays	All extra days eliminated with the exception of Rosh Ha-shono	All extra days eliminated

Jewish Marriage Regulations. Betty studied the chart of European Reform. Then she asked Rabbi Cohen, "What was decided in the case of Jewish marriage and divorce laws?"

"Let's take up the marriage regulations first," he suggested. Hearing no objection he went on.

"Both European and American Reform agreed," he said, "that a legal certificate of death issued by the State enabled the 'Aguno,' the woman whose husband had disappeared, to remarry. Both also permitted the double-ring ceremony in which the bride and groom exchange rings. But once again, American Reform went beyond the decisions reached in Europe."

"In what respect?" Mother wanted to know.

"We have liberalized most of the other Orthodox restrictions," the rabbi answered. "Let me cite a few examples. Whereas the Orthodox list many days during the year on which marriages may not be conducted we prohibit them only on Sabbaths and Jewish holidays. We permit the use of all types of wedding rings contrary to the Orthodox prohibition against those with precious stones. We generally require no *chupo* or canopy, nor do we read the lengthy marriage contract, and we may conduct a wedding without the presence of ten persons."

As the rabbi was speaking, Betty kept writing, and soon her chart was ready.

Problem	Orthodox Practice	Why Reforms Were Needed	European Reform	American Reform
JEWISH MARRIAGE REGULATIONS	Many laws regulating marriage Prohibition of marriage on numerous days	Certain laws worked a special hardship on women With emancipation Jews became subject to civil marriage regulations Many Jewish wedding practices had become outmoded	Laws working a hardship on women abolished Minor reforms made in wedding practices	Laws working a hardship on women abolished Many changes liberalizing Jewish marriage practices Weddings permitted on all days except Sabbaths and Jewish holidays

Jewish Divorce Laws. "And how was the question of Jewish divorce laws settled?" Mother reminded Rabbi Cohen. "European Reform, it seems, reached no decision."

"Which meant that Orthodox practice remained in effect," the rabbi pointed out. "Thus, except in special cases, only the husband was entitled to grant a divorce, and in addition to a civil decree, each Jewish couple was required to obtain a religious divorce from a rabbinical court."

"I'm sure that this was not continued by American Reform," Father declared.

"You're absolutely right," affirmed the rabbi. "At the Philadelphia Rabbinical Conference of 1869 all Jewish divorce laws were promptly abolished and any decree granted by the State and acceptable to both parties was considered sufficient."

Betty's chart on the subject was quickly completed (see next page).

Mourning Customs. "The final problem listed on the chart of European Reform," Betty called out, "is that of Jewish mourning customs."

"May I remind you," Great-Grandfather told the family, "that Orthodox regulations require mourners to make a small cut in one of their garments and to refrain for seven days from shaving, bathing, washing, or wearing shoes. Furthermore, they must remain at home the entire period and spend their waking hours seated on the ground or on low benches."

"European Reform declared these customs meaningless to modern

Problem	Orthodox Practice	Why Reforms Were Needed	European Reform	American Reform
JEWISH DIVORCE LAWS	Religious divorce in addition to a civil decree required Generally only the husband could grant a divorce	In view of civil regulations a Jewish divorce was unnecessary and made for confusion Jewish divorce laws worked a hardship especially on women	No action taken	Practice of religious divorce abolished Civil decree declared satisfactory

Jews," Betty informed them, "and decided that mourners need remain at home for only three days."

"American Reform has taken the same attitude toward Orthodox mourning customs," Rabbi Cohen disclosed. "In this country, most Reform families in mourning remain at home for seven days, but, where necessary, they are permitted to attend to their businesses. On the first evening after the funeral, and generally on each of the two following evenings, a religious service is conducted at home. The family attends Sabbath services at temple to recite the 'Kaddish,' or mourners' prayer, throughout the entire year of mourning, and they commemorate the aniversary of the death each year by attendance at worship and, usually, by a memorial contribution to the synagogue. The dead are also remembered at the special Memorial Services conducted on Yom Kippur afternoon, and, in many congregations, on the last days of Passover and Sukos."

Betty produced this final chart (see next page).

More Differences between European and American Reform. Betty now passed the charts to the rest of the family who looked over each one carefully.

"Hmm," Father observed as he reached the last, "in most instances it doesn't seem as if we went very much beyond European Reform."

"The decisions may appear similar," the rabbi replied, "and certainly the method of careful investigation of the sources of Jewish tradition before arriving at Reform practice was the same, but there are major differences between European and American Reform nevertheless."

"What do you mean by that, Rabbi?" questioned Mother.

"First of all, only American Reform, as in the Pittsburgh Platform, officially declared that the whole of Biblical and Talmudic law was no longer binding upon the Jew. This

Problem	Orthodox Practice	Why Reforms Were Needed	European Reform	American Reform
MOURNING CUSTOMS	Many specific regulations governing mourning A 7-day mourning period maintained	A great number of the mourning regulations were outmoded The 7-day period worked a hardship on the family in cases of financial need	Orthodox mourning practices abolished A 3-day home mourning period prescribed	Orthodox mourning practices abolished A 7-day home mourning period prescribed, with services on the first 3 evenings. However, business may be attended to during the mourning period

made it possible for the movement in the United States to eliminate many practices and beliefs, such as those dealing with ritual purity and Jewish dress, that are totally out of keeping with modern times.

"Secondly, the American Reform movement settled certain religious problems that the leaders in Europe failed to decide—the issues of Jewish marriage and divorce laws, the religious rights of women, the covering of the head at worship, for instance.

"Then, too, in Europe," he went on, "many of the decisions reached by the rabbinical conferences and synods were never carried into general practice. Here and there only a few congregations introduced them. But in the United States, the practices approved by the movement have been adopted by practically every temple.

"Fourthly," he explained, "American Reform went to greater lengths in modernizing already-existing Or-

thodox observances. On the basis of traditional practices, we have produced beautiful ceremonies of naming new-born children in temple, dedicating a new home, kindling the candles at Sabbath eve services, reciting the English Megillah on Purim, and many others.

"Finally," he stated, "we have actually created new ceremonies—the annual Consecration Service on the last day of Sukos, for example, at which all religious school beginners are blessed by the rabbi, and rituals for the installation of a rabbi and new congregational officers, to name but a few. . . ."

"More Reform contributions to American Jewish life," Mother hastened to point out.

Betty Is Promised a Trip. Betty asked the next question. "Who creates these new ceremonies?"

"The Union of American Hebrew Congregations and the Central Conference of American Rabbis," Rabbi Cohen told her.

"Oh, I remember them," Betty recalled. "They're the organizations founded by Rabbi Isaac Mayer Wise —they and the Hebrew Union College," she quickly added.

"How would you like to see for yourself what Rabbi Wise created?" Great-Grandfather inquired.

"Would I!" exclaimed Betty enthusiastically. "But, how . . . ?"

"I think that can be arranged," he assured her, and turning to Father he asked, "Aren't you planning a business trip East soon?"

"Why yes," answered Father. "I'm leaving here Tuesday by car for Cincinnati and New York."

"Well, prepare yourself for extra passengers," said Great-Grandfather. "Betty and I are going along."

QUESTIONS FOR DISCUSSION

1. Compared with European Reform what advances did American Reform make in religious practices?
2. How do American and European Reform differ in the matter of praying with covered heads, observance of the Sabbath, extra days of the Jewish holidays, and Jewish mourning customs?
3. How do American and European Reform differ in Jewish marriage and divorce regulations and religious rights for women?
4. In what respect does your temple agree in its practices with the decisions of European Reform?

5. What is the present-day American Reform attitude toward the use of Hebrew in worship, the use of instrumental music and the mixed choir in the synagogue?
6. What are some of the principal differences between present-day Reform and Orthodox practices?

SUGGESTED ACTIVITIES

1. Prepare a class booklet on the subject: "A Guide to Reform Practice in Our Temple."
2. In two parallel columns write up a newspaper account of an Orthodox and Reform wedding.
3. Create a series of posters which illustrate the major differences between Orthodox and Reform practices.

ADDITIONAL READINGS FOR PUPILS

LEVINGER, LEE J., *A History of the Jews in the U.S.*, pp. 238-242.

References for the Teacher

FREEHOF, S. B., *Reform Jewish Practice.*

Jewish Encyclopedia, "Reform Judaism from the Point of View of the Reform Jew," Vol. 10, pp. 347-352.

POOL, DAVID DE SOLA, *The American Jew—a Composite Portrait,* edited by Oscar I. Janowsky, "Judaism and the Synagogue," pp. 28-55 (Reform, Conservative and Orthodox Judaism).

SCHWARTZMAN, S. D., *Reform Judaism in the Making,* Chap. 15, "The Practices of Modern Reform Judaism."

SCHWARZ, JACOB D., *Reform Judaism, Essays by Alumni of the Hebrew Union College,* "Reform Jewish Practice," pp. 221-249.

15. BETTY TAKES A TRIP

Off to Cincinnati! Betty could hardly wait for Tuesday to come but finally the morning arrived. It was still very early when Father, Great-Grandfather and she piled into the family car, and soon the automobile was pulling away from the house.

"We're off to Cincinnati!" Betty shouted excitedly.

They traveled for several hours, and by early afternoon they reached the outskirts of Cincinnati.

"We're almost there," Father announced. "Suppose I drop you off downtown where I have my business appointments."

"Fine," Great-Grandfather answered. "We can catch a trolley-bus from there to the Hebrew Union College-Jewish Institute of Religion."

A half-hour later Betty and Great-Grandfather got out of the car. They arranged to meet Father for dinner and bade him good-bye.

In a few moments they were board-ing a trolley-bus for the Clifton section of Cincinnati. In about twenty minutes they passed the campus of the University of Cincinnati and two blocks later got off in front of the Hebrew Union College-Jewish Institute of Religion.

On the Campus of the College-Institute. As Betty caught her first glimpse of the spacious campus and the five attractive brick buildings, she was very much impressed.

Great-Grandfather led her directly to the dormitory where one of the students volunteered to escort them through the building. He conducted them into the large lobby and the attractive dining-room. They then visited several of the students' quarters.

"This dormitory," their guide told them, "was presented by the National Federation of Temple Sister-hoods in 1925. Nearly one hundred students live here."

"What entrance requirements does

Above is an aerial view of the buildings and campus of the Hebrew Union College–Jewish Institute of Religion in Cincinnati, Ohio.

At the left is a photograph of the New York School of the Hebrew Union College–Jewish Institute of Religion.

the College-Institute have?" asked Great-Grandfather.

"To be admitted to the full rabbinical course of study," the student explained, "one must be a university graduate, possess good character and capacity for study, and have a satisfactory knowledge of Jewish history, beliefs, ceremonies, Hebrew and the Bible. Those who do not have sufficient Jewish knowledge are given special training to prepare them for admission to the rabbinical program."

"And how long does the student remain here?" Betty asked him.

"He spends from four to six years taking courses in all fields of Jewish knowledge—Bible, Talmud, history, religious education, Jewish music, and many other subjects. When he completes his work satisfactorily, he is then ordained as a rabbi."

"It sounds to me," observed Betty, "as though all a student at the College-Institute does is study."

"Oh, no," he quickly replied. "Our students have many other interests. We take an active part in Jewish activities in Cincinnati and nearby cities; we conduct youth groups, teach in religious schools and even serve as student-rabbis. And here at the College-Institute we participate in athletic, social, and literary activities. Many of us also carry on special work such as research on projects and preparing College-Institute publications through the Student Placement Bureau."

They walked outside to the separate building at the rear which turned out to be a fully-equipped gymnasium with a swimming pool. From here they made their way to the library which really consisted of two structures connected by a covered walk. The smaller one was the Bernheim Library, headquarters of the American Jewish Archives and also of the Museum with more than 10,000 Jewish ceremonial and art objects. The larger building was the new library built in 1931, and they browsed through its spacious reading rooms and some of the rare-book rooms.

"We have over 125,000 Jewish books here," the librarian informed them, "including some of the finest collections of old manuscripts, Jewish music, and writings concerning the great Jewish philosopher, Baruch Spinoza."

They now turned to enter the last of the five buildings, the Administration Building, where the classes were conducted. There, in the corridor in front of the beautiful College Chapel, Betty spied a bronze bust of the founder, Isaac Mayer Wise.

Soon they were ushered into the office of the President, and Great-Grandfather explained their mission.

The Work of the College-Institute. "Delighted to have you visit us," the President greeted them with a warm smile. After they were seated, he turned to them and said, "Tell me, what would you like to know about the College-Institute?"

Great-Grandfather asked the first question. "Does the College-Institute only prepare rabbis?"

"By no means," answered the President. "We are engaged in training university graduates as directors of religious education for many Reform congregations and they receive a Master's degree when they complete their work."

"Is this program open to women, too?" Betty questioned.

"Yes," the President replied, "and so is most of our other graduate work. We offer a Doctor of Philosophy degree to those who wish to engage in Jewish studies at the school. In addition to Jewish students, we have a number of Christian ministers who are enrolled in this program. We also award the Doctor of Hebrew Letters degree to our own graduates who pursue an intensive course of study while remaining in their own communities. But our principal task remains that of training rabbis."

"I didn't realize the College-Institute offered so many different types of programs," confessed Great-Grandfather.

"We do many other things," said the President. "For instance, in co-operation with the Union of American Hebrew Congregations, we maintain the Hebrew Union School of Education for the training of religious school teachers and directors,

the School of Jewish Sacred Music for preparing temple cantors, as well as a College of Jewish Studies in Los Angeles. And our professors are often called upon to lecture to teachers and congregational and community groups. Then, too, we have the American Jewish Archives. . . ."

"What is that?" Betty asked.

"The Archives," he answered, "collects and preserves important records of American Jewry. Diaries and letters of prominent American Jews, congregational minute-books, community records, and the like are classified and made available to those who are writing the history of the American Jew and his contributions to this country."

"I have only one other question," Betty stated. "Where did the College-Institute get its 'double' name?"

The President laughed. "Lots of people ask that question," he commented. "You see, originally there were two Reform rabbinical seminaries in the United States—the Hebrew Union College *and* the Jewish Institute of Religion. The College is America's oldest rabbinical seminary today and was founded in Cincinnati in 1875 through the efforts of Rabbi Isaac Mayer Wise and his newly-formed Union of American Hebrew Congregations. The Institute was created in 1922 in New York by Dr. Stephen S. Wise, an outstanding American Reform leader. In 1950 these schools were merged, and the combined seminary, therefore, car-

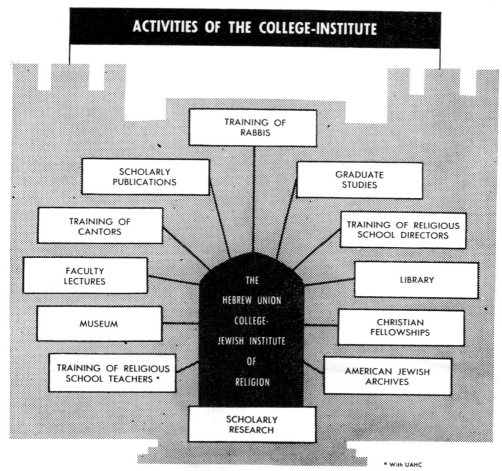

ACTIVITIES OF THE COLLEGE-INSTITUTE

TRAINING OF RABBIS

SCHOLARLY PUBLICATIONS

GRADUATE STUDIES

TRAINING OF CANTORS

TRAINING OF RELIGIOUS SCHOOL DIRECTORS

FACULTY LECTURES

THE HEBREW UNION COLLEGE-JEWISH INSTITUTE OF RELIGION

LIBRARY

MUSEUM

CHRISTIAN FELLOWSHIPS

TRAINING OF RELIGIOUS SCHOOL TEACHERS *

AMERICAN JEWISH ARCHIVES

SCHOLARLY RESEARCH

* With UAHC

ries both names, or 'College-Institute' for short. While a Liberal rabbinical school was opened in Paris in 1955, the College-Institute remains the world's chief Reform seminary, with students coming from countries as far away as Turkey and the Union of South Africa."

"Then does the College-Institute run two schools, one in Cincinnati and one in New York?" Betty asked.

"That's right," responded the President. "Our New York school operates in its original headquarters at 40 West Sixty-eighth Street, and it is very much a part of our rabbinical training program. The Hebrew Union School of Education and the School of Jewish Sacred Music are also conducted there."

"How many students does the College-Institute graduate?" Great-Grandfather wanted to know.

"More than 800," the President

answered, "and they serve congregations in Canada, England, Panama, South Africa, Cuba, and Israel as well as throughout the United States. Some of our rabbis have headed important American and world Jewish causes, such as the Joint Distribution Committee, the Zionist Organization of America, the Hebrew University in Israel, and many, many others. Numbers of our graduates also serve as chaplains in the armed forces, as directors of Hillel Foundations on the campuses of leading universities, and as leaders of various Jewish community agencies."

Great-Grandfather looked at his watch and saw that it was time to leave. He and Betty rose and thanked the President. They bade him goodbye and left the office.

"That was most interesting," Betty told Great-Grandfather as they walked down the main steps of the College-Institute campus. When they reached the street she asked, "Where to now?"

"Well, since we can't attend a session of the Central Conference of American Rabbis because it meets only once a year," he responded, "we'll do the next best thing. Suppose we meet with its President who happens to be the rabbi of a Cincinnati congregation. . . ."

The Central Conference of American Rabbis. In a short while they arrived at the home of the President of the Central Conference of American Rabbis and were seated in his study. Great-Grandfather explained why they had come.

"Fine," the President said. "Now what information about the Conference would you like to have?"

"How many members do you have?" questioned Betty.

"More than 600," he replied, "and practically all are functioning rabbis. We meet in convention in a different city each year."

"What, exactly, is the work of the Conference?" Betty asked.

"We do many things," the President told her. "Since 1894, we have written and published the *Union Prayerbook* which is used by practically every Reform congregation. We create choir music for our temples and publish the *Union Hymnal*. Together with the Union, we originate new Jewish ceremonies, supervise the writing of textbooks, aid in furthering religious activities at universities, participate in projects of social justice and peace, maintain a pension fund for rabbis, decide issues of religion in relationship to the State, and many other joint activities. But most important of all, we decide upon questions of Reform principles, practices, and beliefs. . . ."

"Like adopting 'The Guiding Principles of Reform Judaism'?" Betty suggested.

"That's right," the President nodded. "Ever since the Conference was organized by Isaac Mayer Wise in 1889 in Detroit, we've had to set-

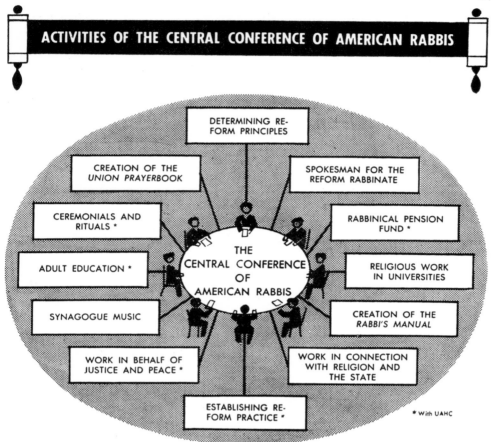

ACTIVITIES OF THE CENTRAL CONFERENCE OF AMERICAN RABBIS

DETERMINING RE-FORM PRINCIPLES

CREATION OF THE UNION PRAYERBOOK

SPOKESMAN FOR THE REFORM RABBINATE

CEREMONIALS AND RITUALS *

RABBINICAL PENSION FUND *

ADULT EDUCATION *

THE CENTRAL CONFERENCE OF AMERICAN RABBIS

RELIGIOUS WORK IN UNIVERSITIES

SYNAGOGUE MUSIC

CREATION OF THE RABBI'S MANUAL

WORK IN BEHALF OF JUSTICE AND PEACE *

WORK IN CONNECTION WITH RELIGION AND THE STATE

ESTABLISHING RE-FORM PRACTICE *

* With UAHC

tle questions that arise about Reform practice. We appoint committees to study and report on all such matters.

"Finally," the President explained, "the Conference also represents the Reform rabbinate in many national and international organizations that serve in behalf of major Jewish activities and important general world causes."

They spoke together for a while longer, but since it was growing late, Great-Grandfather and Betty had to excuse themselves in order to keep their appointment with Father.

As they walked to the corner to catch the trolley-bus downtown, Betty said to Great-Grandfather, "It's simply amazing how many organizations Isaac Mayer Wise founded. His name keeps being mentioned every time we discuss one of the Reform agencies. First there was the College-Institute . . . then the Central Conference of American Rabbis. . . ."

"That's not the order in which they were formed," Great-Grandfather pointed out. "First came the Union of American Hebrew Congregations. . . ."

"That's right," Betty recalled. "Is the Union of American Hebrew Congregations located in Cincinnati, too?"

"No," Great-Grandfather responded, "the Union's headquarters were here for more than seventy years, but in 1948 it was decided that they should be moved to New York."

"Won't we get to visit the Union?" asked Betty.

"Certainly," Great-Grandfather declared. "We're practically on our way since we're leaving for New York tomorrow. . . ."

The House of Living Judaism. It was more than a full day's drive from Cincinnati to New York, and Betty, Great-Grandfather, and Father were exhausted when they finally arrived at their hotel late that night. But after a good night's sleep and a hearty breakfast they all felt refreshed. Soon all three of them were making their way in the bright sunshine across Central Park.

"There it is!" exclaimed Father, "the House of Living Judaism."

"That's the headquarters of the Union of American Hebrew Congregations, Betty," Great-Grandfather explained.

Betty looked where he was pointing and there on the corner of Fifth Avenue and Sixty-fifth Street was a beautiful seven-story, white limestone building. Across the front it prominently bore the inscription from the Book of Leviticus, "Love thy neighbor as thyself."

Soon they found themselves in the marble lobby with its attractive ceremonial display cases, the exhibit of Union publications and the lovely Chapel. Beautiful plaques illustrating the various Jewish holidays decorated the upper portion of each wall. After they looked over the lobby thoroughly they took the elevator to the seventh floor.

Great-Grandfather announced to the receptionist who they were and why they had come, and she invited them to meet with the President of the Union.

As they walked toward his office, Father remarked to the receptionist that he considered the House of Living Judaism one of the most beautiful buildings he had ever seen. "When was it built?" he asked.

"It was dedicated in October of 1951," she answered. "It was the gift of the National Federation of Temple Sisterhoods and Dr. Albert A. Berg, a prominent New York surgeon. That is why it is also called 'The Moritz and Josephine Berg Memorial,' in honor of Dr. Berg's parents," she explained.

Why a Union of Congregations? The President arose as they entered his office and shook hands with them.

The Berg Memorial–House of Living Judaism, home of the Union of American Hebrew Congregations and its affiliates in New York City.

After they were seated, Great-Grandfather explained that they had come to New York especially to see the House of Living Judaism and find out more about the Union of American Hebrew Congregations. "I'd be grateful to you," he said to the President, "if you would tell us about the Union and its activities."

"I'll be happy to," he answered. "Suppose I start with its founding."

"It was organized by Isaac Mayer Wise, wasn't it?" Betty asked.

"That's right," he replied. "Rabbi Wise had not been in this country very long before he came to the conclusion that all Reform congregations should join together in one national organization. . . ."

"And what were to be some of its functions?" questioned Great-Grandfather.

"Not only to publicize the ideas of Reform Judaism and stimulate its growth, but to perform many necessary services which no single congregation could undertake," he said. "A union of congregations, moreover, would be able to organize and maintain a rabbinical seminary for the training of American Reform rabbis."

"How long did it take before the Union was finally organized?" asked Great-Grandfather.

"Twenty-seven years from the time that Rabbi Wise first came to America," he declared. "On July 8, 1873, at his invitation, twenty-eight congregations sent delegates to Cincinnati where they agreed to establish the Union of American Hebrew Congregations. By 1900 it had eighty-eight member congregations, and in 1955 there were over 500."

"How many Reform members does that represent?" Betty inquired.

"About 170,000 temple memberships," he stated. "Since each membership usually represents an entire family, and since there are many who are not actual temple members but are affiliated only with our Sisterhoods, Brotherhoods and Youth groups, we estimate that there are at least 700,000 Reform Jews in America."

"That's about one-seventh of all the Jews in the United States," Great-Grandfather observed.

The Activities of the Union. "Suppose we go and visit some of the departments of the Union," the President suggested. As they rose and walked through the corridor with him, Betty raised another question. "What are some of the things the Union does?" she asked the President of the Union.

"It tries to aid its member congregations in every possible way," he answered. "Throughout the country, for example, the Union has a number of Regional Directors who meet with local congregations and assist them in improving their religious schools, increasing attendance at worship, strengthening their Sisterhoods, Brotherhoods and Youth

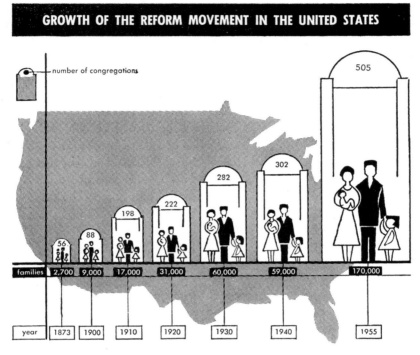

GROWTH OF THE REFORM MOVEMENT IN THE UNITED STATES

number of congregations

		56	88	198	222	282	302		505
families		2,700	9,000	17,000	31,000	60,000	59,000		170,000
year		1873	1900	1910	1920	1930	1940		1955

groups, and providing every kind of practical information. They also organize new Reform congregations and religious schools in the areas that they serve.

"But the Union carries on many other projects," he went on. "We publish and distribute a series of popular pamphlets on Judaism which presents over thirty different aspects of our religion. 'What Do Jews Believe?' 'Judaism and Democracy,' 'What Is the Talmud?' 'The Jewish Prayer Book'—are some of the titles. Thousands of Jews and Christians have written us that these book-

lets are the best that they have ever read on the subject."

"And you also publish the interesting magazine, *American Judaism,* which is sent to all members of Reform congregations, Sisterhoods and Brotherhoods," Father mentioned.

"Yes," the President declared, "that's another informational service of the Union. *American Judaism* presents special articles and features of interest to Reform members and contains sections devoted to the work and activities of the Sisterhoods and Brotherhoods."

"Would you mind telling us how

the Union encourages the practice of Reform ceremonials?" Great-Grandfather requested.

"Now that we're at the office of the Department of Synagogue Activities I'll ask the Director to give you that information," he answered.

They entered the office and were greeted by the Director. The President repeated Great-Grandfather's question.

"My department promotes ceremonial observance in many ways," the Director explained. "For instance, we prepare experimental services and produce ceremonial objects like the magnificent bronze Chanuko Menorah and the beautiful English Megillah for Purim. We even supply special certificates for commemorating important religious occasions in an individual's life, such as Bar Mitzvah, Confirmation, and marriage."

Great-Grandfather turned to Betty. "Do you see," he told her, "in how many different ways the Union of American Hebrew Congregations advances the cause of Judaism?"

"But, wait," the Director of Synagogue Activities interrupted. "I've only mentioned a few of our services. If, for instance, a congregation decides to erect a new temple, my department advises it on building plans. If a congregation wishes to stimulate singing at worship, we assist them. In fact, we furnish every sort of synagogue aid from informing the rabbi on sources of temple supplies to as-

sisting the congregational treasurer in setting up his financial records."

They thanked the Director for the information and left his office. As they headed for the elevator Betty turned to the President of the Union and asked, "Don't you also publish our religious school books?"

"Yes, indeed," he replied vigorously, "and I'm taking you to the Director of that department right now to tell you all about it." They made their way to the third floor and he introduced Betty, Father, and Great-Grandfather to the Union's Director of Education.

Betty repeated her question to him. "Isn't it your office which publishes our religious school books?"

"That's one of the most important activities of my department," the Director answered. "We've published more than 400 different items for religious school and adult education, and distributed nearly two million copies to a thousand schools throughout the world. We also produce interesting movies, filmstrips and recordings as aids to Jewish education and prepare special materials for pre-school children, parents, and teachers. In fact, in many sections of the country we even assist in conducting colleges and classes for the training of religious school teachers."

"The Union's textbooks and teacher-training program are among Reform's finest contributions to the American Jewish community," declared Great-Grandfather as they left the Department of Education.

"As you can see," the President remarked, "we try to assist our congregations in every way—through conferences of temple presidents and secretaries, regional congregational conventions, and the work of many national committees of the Union. At the request of local temples, we even provide well-qualified authorities on Judaism to conduct Institutes for Christian ministers."

"I never realized the Union did so much," confessed Father.

Sisterhoods—Brotherhoods—Temple Youth. "But you've seen only part of the Union," the President said. "There are the Sisterhoods. . . ."

"That's the organization to which Mother belongs," Betty broke in.

"And in addition to the work which Mother's Sisterhood performs for your temple," the President pointed out, "it also participates in the national and international activities of the National Federation of Temple Sisterhoods of which it is a member."

He guided them toward the lady who was just coming down the corridor.

"I want you to meet the Executive Director of the National Federation of Temple Sisterhoods," he said as he introduced the Friedbergs. "They would like to know more about your organization," he told her.

"First of all," she explained, "we came into existence in 1913 to assist in promoting the work and program of every local Sisterhood, and we now consist of more than 500 Reform women's groups with over 100,000 members.

"Then, too," she continued, "through the sale of our Uniongrams we aid the students of the College-Institute and assist the Union in publishing some of its books. In 1925, we presented the Hebrew Union College with its attractive dormitory, and we contributed a great deal of the funds to erect this House of Living Judaism. The National Federation of Temple Sisterhoods carries on many more activities. To name a few, our organization performs outstanding work in behalf of the Jewish blind by publishing many books in braille; and we cooperate in numbers of ways with national and international organizations that strive for a better, more peaceful world."

"NFTS also publishes the very attractive Sisterhood calendar each year," the President added.

The Executive Director of the National Federation of Temple Brotherhoods joined the group. "If you're explaining the work of the Union," he said, "don't forget the Brotherhoods."

"And what do they do?" Betty turned to him.

"Our main national project," he told her, "is the Jewish Chautauqua Society which provides courses and lectures on Judaism at over 500

American colleges and universities each year. In addition, our organization which was founded in 1923 assists the local Temple Brotherhood, promotes temple attendance, and produces many fine Jewish art and ceremonial creations. Today, the NFTB comprises over 315 temple men's clubs with a total membership of more than 53,000."

"Didn't you mention that the Union also has a youth organization?" Great-Grandfather asked the President.

"Indeed we have," he assured Great-Grandfather, "and I'll have you meet the Executive Director of the National Federation of Temple Youth." In a few moments he had them in the Director's office. "Won't you please tell my friends about the program of NFTY?" he requested.

"I'll be very happy to," the Director replied. "Our organization," he explained, "has more than 350 young people's groups with more than 13,-000 members. We serve as the clearing-house for all Reform youth programs and activities—religious, educational, social, and interfaith."

"What special projects have you?" Father inquired.

"Quite a few," the Director stated. "Among them are the Week-End Camp Conclaves conducted in all parts of the country, and the NFTY Summer Institutes at the Union-owned summer camps at which Reform youth gather to discuss vital Jewish subjects, and participate in outdoor religious services, choral, dramatic, and educational programs. We also publish a monthly magazine, *The Messenger,* for all of our members, and a specialized publication, *The Youth Leader,* for all persons who are interested in Jewish youth work."

"In Union There Is Strength!"
"With such a Union," Betty declared, "it's no wonder that American Reform made so much greater progress than the movement in Europe." She paused. "But I'm still curious about one thing. Who runs the Union?"

"Its member congregations," answered the President. "Every two years," he explained, "we hold a national convention—the Biennial Assembly, we call it—of representatives of all Union congregations. These delegates elect the Officers and Board of the Union and determine its future program and policies. Actually," he explained to her, "we are a union of independent congregations. Each temple decides its own affairs; the Union merely serves and represents it. In this way the organization remains democratic and, at the same time, strengthens the Reform movement."

When the President finished speaking, Great-Grandfather, Father, and Betty thanked him for his kindness and left him. "You know," Betty told Father as they rode in the elevator, "while the President was speaking,

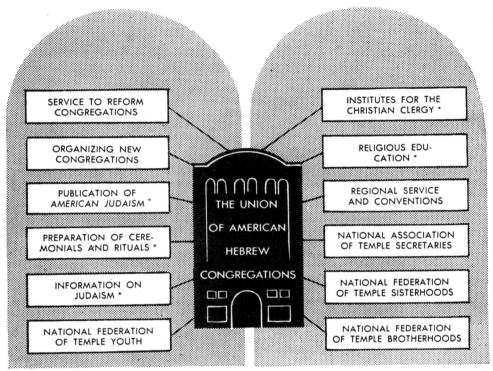

ACTIVITIES OF THE UNION OF AMERICAN HEBREW CONGREGATIONS

SERVICE TO REFORM CONGREGATIONS

ORGANIZING NEW CONGREGATIONS

PUBLICATION OF AMERICAN JUDAISM *

PREPARATION OF CEREMONIALS AND RITUALS *

INFORMATION ON JUDAISM *

NATIONAL FEDERATION OF TEMPLE YOUTH

THE UNION OF AMERICAN HEBREW CONGREGATIONS

INSTITUTES FOR THE CHRISTIAN CLERGY *

RELIGIOUS EDUCATION *

REGIONAL SERVICE AND CONVENTIONS

NATIONAL ASSOCIATION OF TEMPLE SECRETARIES

NATIONAL FEDERATION OF TEMPLE SISTERHOODS

NATIONAL FEDERATION OF TEMPLE BROTHERHOODS

* With CCAR

I kept thinking of the slogan, 'In union there is strength!' "

"That's certainly true in the case of American Reform Judaism," Father agreed.

They turned to leave the House of Living Judaism and started back to the hotel. Betty sighed. "Well, that's the last of the important Reform organizations," she said.

To her surprise Great-Grand-Grandfather corrected her. "No," he told her. "There's one more—the World Union for Progressive Judaism."

A World Reform Organization. "What," questioned Betty, "is the World Union for Progressive Judaism?"

"The organization which unites the Reform movement throughout the world," came his reply.

"I hadn't heard of that one before, either," Father admitted. "When was it organized?"

"It was founded in 1926 under the leadership of Miss Lily Montagu, Rabbi Israel Mattuck, and Dr. Claude G. Montefiore, all prominent Reform leaders of England. On July 10-12 of that year, Reform representatives from England, the United States, Germany, Czechoslovakia, France, Sweden, and India met in London for a conference, and there they formed the World Union for Progressive Judaism as a permanent organization."

"For what purpose?" Betty wanted to know.

"To promote Reform Judaism throughout the world," said Great-Grandfather. "At its second meeting in 1928," he disclosed, "the organization agreed upon two principal aims: (1) to encourage the growth of Reform in every country and insure cooperation between already existing Reform groups in various lands; and (2) to preserve Judaism by adjusting it to modern conditions and stimulating all Jews to participate in religious life."

"How has it attempted to carry out these purposes?" Father asked Great-Grandfather.

"It has had considerable success in establishing new Reform congregations in many countries," he replied. "Thanks to its work, there are now active Reform movements in Holland, Australia, South Africa, Israel, India, South America, and other

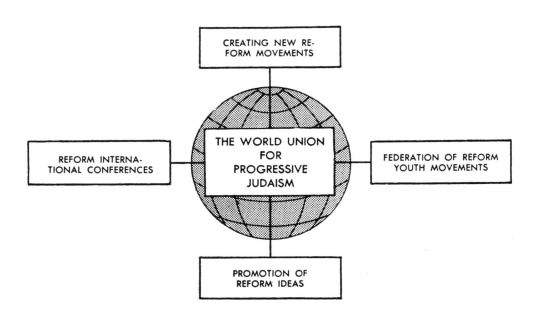

ACTIVITIES OF THE WORLD UNION FOR PROGRESSIVE JUDAISM

CREATING NEW RE-FORM MOVEMENTS

REFORM INTERNA-TIONAL CONFERENCES

THE WORLD UNION FOR PROGRESSIVE JUDAISM

FEDERATION OF REFORM YOUTH MOVEMENTS

PROMOTION OF REFORM IDEAS

lands; and it has helped establish a Liberal seminary in Paris. Meeting every two years to consider Reform progress and plan further activities, it also maintains a world Federation of Reform Youth organizations."

A Visit to the New York School. By now they reached the hotel. Father went off to attend to his business downtown, and Great-Grandfather and Betty decided to spend the rest of the day visiting the New York school of the College-Institute and some of the magnificent Reform temples of the city.

They made their way across Central Park to 40 West Sixty-eighth Street where they came upon the attractive Tudor style building which houses the New York school. Here they met several members of the faculty and attended a class conducted for the rabbinical students. Then they were shown through the school's fine library of more than 65,000 volumes.

"The New York school," their guide reminded them, "was originally established in 1922 as the Jewish Institute of Religion. Its founder and the President until the school was merged with the Hebrew Union College was Dr. Stephen S. Wise, one of the most forceful leaders in American and world Jewish life. Rabbi of the Free Synagogue in New York, he was a vigorous defender of Jewish rights and an outstanding figure in many important Jewish movements including Zionism and the American Jewish Congress."

As they went through the building, they heard strains of Jewish music coming from one of the rooms. "This is also the headquarters of the Hebrew Union School of Education and School of Jewish Sacred Music," their guide told them.

"What are they?" Betty wanted to know.

"The first is the school that trains religious school teachers and principals mainly for the New York area Reform congregations. The second prepares young men to serve as cantors in synagogues throughout the country, and those who successfully complete the course receive the Bachelor of Sacred Music degree."

They finished their tour of the building, and Great-Grandfather and Betty thanked their guide and left. Then they spent several hours visiting a number of well-known New York Reform synagogues. It was almost dark when they finally returned to the hotel.

"Wait 'Til I See Mildred!" The next day they were speeding homeward. As they rode along, Father turned to Betty and asked, "How did you enjoy your visit to Cincinnati and New York?"

"Very much," she answered enthusiastically. "It was exciting to see the progress that Reform has made." She sighed. "Just think, we've got a union of Reform congregations, one combined Reform seminary, a conference of Reform rabbis, and—something I didn't know—a world Reform organization!"

"Reform certainly is moving forward, isn't it?" Father observed.

"So much so," asserted Great-Grandfather, "that both the Orthodox and Conservative groups have patterned their own religious organizations after Reform. They each have their unions of congregations, organizations of synagogue women and men, conferences of rabbis, and seminaries. . . ."

Great-Grandfather hadn't finished his sentence when Betty blurted out, "Just wait 'til I see Mildred!"

"Mildred?" Father asked, somewhat puzzled. "Why Mildred?"

"She's the one who took me to the Orthodox synagogue last Saturday and kept asking me lots of questions about Reform. I didn't know too many of the answers then," she admitted. "But," she promised significantly, "just wait until I see her next time. . . ."

In connection with this chapter, the class will want to see the motion picture, "The Union in Action" and the filmstrip, "Within the Family of Liberal Judaism." Both may be secured through the Union of American Hebrew Congregations.

QUESTIONS FOR DISCUSSION

1. How does one become a Reform rabbi?
2. In what ways does the Hebrew Union College-Jewish Institute of Religion aid the Reform movement?
3. How does the work of the Central Conference of American Rabbis promote the development of American Reform?
4. In what ways does your temple benefit from the activities of the Union of American Hebrew Congregations?
5. Why should American Reform Jews be concerned with the spread of the movement throughout the world?
6. In comparison with the movement in Europe, how has the development of Reform organizations in America benefited the movement here?

SUGGESTED ACTIVITIES

1. Invite the rabbi of your temple to discuss his training for the rabbinate.
2. Draw up a chart of your congregation's activities and indicate those areas in which it receives assistance from national Reform organizations.
3. Prepare a pamphlet on the work of the Hebrew Union College-Jewish Institute of Religion and the Union of American Hebrew Congregations for use in connection with a school fund-raising campaign for these organizations.

ADDITIONAL READINGS FOR PUPILS

ALOFSIN, DOROTHY, *The Stream of Jewish Life,* pp. 29-32, 34-44, 177-180.

FEUER, LEON I. and AZRIEL EISENBERG, *Jewish Literature Since the Bible, II,* pp. 187-190.

LEVINGER, LEE J., *A History of the Jews in the United States,* pp. 393-399, 416-417.

SOLOFF, MORDECAI I., *How the Jewish People Lives Today,* Chap. XVI, pp. 213-215.

References for the Teacher

COHON, SAMUEL S., *Publications of the American Jewish Historical Society,* September, 1950, "The History of the Hebrew Union College," pp. 17-55.

Jewish Encyclopedia, "Conferences of American Rabbis," Vol. 4, pp. 215-217; "Hebrew Union College," Vol. 6, p. 311; "Union of American Hebrew Congregations," Vol. 12, pp. 344-345.

MASSERMAN, PAUL and MAX BAKER, *The Jews Come to America,* pp. 187-197 (founding of the Union, College and Conference).

PHILIPSON, DAVID, *Centenary Papers and Others,* "The Principles and Achievements of the Central Conference of American Rabbis," pp. 191-228. (Also found in *Central Conference of American Rabbis Yearbook,* Vol. 23.)

——, *The Reform Movement in Judaism,* pp. 357-358 (founding of the Conference); pp. 377-381 (founding of the Union, College and Institute); pp. 428-434 (founding of the World Union).

SCHWARTZMAN, SYLVAN D., *Reform Judaism in the Making,* Chap. 16, "How Reform Is Organized."

Universal Jewish Encyclopedia, "Central Conference of American Rabbis," Vol. 3, pp. 88-92; "Hebrew Union College," Vol. 5, pp. 282-283; "Jewish Institute of Religion," Vol. 6, pp. 132-133; "Union of American Hebrew Congregations," Vol. 10, pp. 344-345; "Stephen S. Wise," Vol. 10, pp. 543-544; "World Union for Progressive Judaism," Vol. 10, pp. 575-576.

16. SO THIS IS REFORM JUDAISM!

Betty Keeps Her Promise. It was Friday night in the Friedberg home. How beautiful the table looked with its snow-white cloth, sparkling dishes, and glistening silver! As the family stood about the table, everyone had the feeling that Shabos was indeed something special, like celebrating an important holiday.

The family stood quietly as Mother kindled the candles and Father recited the Kiddush. Betty, as usual, was given the privilege of reciting the "Motsi" over the twisted loaf, and after everyone was seated, Great-Grandfather led them in singing some of the delightful Sabbath songs. Now, all too soon for Betty, dinner and the final grace were over. But it was already 7:30 by her watch and time for the family to leave for temple.

"Will you please drop me off at Mildred's?" Betty requested of Father.

"What!" Mother asked in surprise. "Aren't you going to temple tonight?"

"Of course," Betty reassured her. "But tonight," she explained, "I've got to call for a guest. I'm bringing Mildred."

"So," observed Great-Grandfather, "I see you've kept your promise to tell her about Reform."

"Not yet," Betty answered. "I've simply invited her to come to temple with me, but I'll keep the rest of my promise afterward." And with that Betty excused herself to get ready for temple. Soon Father let her off in front of Mildred's house.

Mildred Attends a Temple Service. "It seems mighty strange to be going to Friday evening services after dark," Mildred commented as the two girls began their walk to temple.

"Our late service makes it possible for whole families to attend Sabbath worship together," Betty pointed out. "That's part of Reform's attempt to meet the needs of modern Jews."

Mildred didn't reply but Betty felt that she had been impressed by her answer.

In a short while, the girls entered the temple, and immediately Mildred sensed a difference. Although the service had not as yet begun, the people were meditating quietly to the soft strains of the organ. No one spoke or even stirred; the atmosphere was one of prayerfulness and reverence.

But she noted other differences as well. There was no separation of men and women; instead, entire families were seated together. And she was equally surprised to see that the men did not wear hats.

The girls were no sooner seated than the congregation joined with the choir of men and women in singing the lovely "Sholom Aleichem."

Mildred couldn't restrain herself from whispering to Betty. "You use an organ and mixed choir at services!" she said with a certain astonishment.

"Of course," Betty whispered back. "They're part of Reform Judaism's efforts to beautify the service."

The rabbi, wearing a handsome black robe draped with a talis-like stole, came to the pulpit and commenced reading the service from the *Union Prayerbook.* Mildred noted that both English and Hebrew were used in temple worship and she found all of the Hebrew prayers very familiar. Now and then she glanced around the temple. It was practically like the Orthodox synagogue except that it had no raised platform in the center.

As the service proceeded the rabbi announced that he would continue with the Torah ritual. Mildred confided to Betty that at the shul the Torah was taken out at night only on Simchas Torah and Yom Kippur.

"We read the Torah every Friday night," Betty replied. "Many Reform congregations have introduced this practice because it enables people who can't get to temple on Saturday to hear the weekly Torah portion."

Mildred watched two members of the congregation come up to the pulpit to recite the Torah blessings, and immediately after the rabbi read the Hebrew passage for that Sabbath he translated it into English. With the return of the Torah to the Ark, the rabbi came to the pulpit to deliver the sermon which Mildred followed with considerable interest.

At the conclusion of the sermon the congregation joined in the recitation of the Adoration. At temple, Mildred observed, the rabbi pronounced the Kaddish for the mourners while at the shul each mourner rose and recited it himself. The congregational hymn and rabbi's blessing ended the service, and the members now greeted one another with "Good Shabos." Instead of leaving the temple, however, the congregation headed for the Social Hall.

"Where is everyone going?" Mildred asked Betty. "Isn't the service over?"

"We hold a Sabbath social after

Friday night services," Betty informed her. "We gather in the Social Hall where we have refreshments and conduct discussions or sing Hebrew songs." Betty paused, and then she added, "That's a Sabbath custom in most temples."

It was nearly ten o'clock before the two girls left the Social Hall, and on the way home, Mildred told Betty how much she had enjoyed being at temple. "That Sabbath social," she commented, "certainly helps to make Friday night a real Shabos evening."

"And how did you like the service?" Betty asked.

"Very much," Mildred admitted. "The music and the English prayers were beautiful, and everyone prayed so quietly. But of course," she hastened to add, "there was much that was different from our services at the shul."

"I'm happy that you could come with me," Betty said to her friend.

"I'm glad, too. I'd never been to a Reform temple before."

Where Did Reform Come From? The two girls walked along quietly for a while. Finally Mildred broke the silence.

"Tell me, Betty," she asked, "where did Reform Judaism come from?"

"From Orthodox Judaism," Betty said simply.

"If that's true," Mildred wanted to know, "how do you explain the many differences—men and women seated together, the use of the organ and mixed choir, men without hats, and all the rest?"

"It's a long story," Betty told her. The girls had now reached Mildred's house.

"It's still early. Let's sit on the porch," Mildred suggested, "and you can tell me about it."

Both girls sat down on the porch swing. "There's much more to it than this," Betty began, "but briefly, this is the story of Reform Judaism. . . ."

Before the Beginning of Reform. "Less than two hundred years ago," Betty commenced, "practically all Jews were forced to live together in ghettos. The ignorant people of those days persecuted the Jews mainly because they refused to give up their Judaism, and they made all kinds of fantastic charges against them. Frequently, too, cruel mobs would break into the ghetto and attack its Jewish inhabitants.

"Moreover," she continued, "the Jew found himself excluded from the life outside the ghetto by the feudal system and the many discriminations against him. Our people, you see, were not considered citizens of the countries in which they lived.

"It was natural, therefore, that within the ghetto Jews should have created their own separate community. In addition to schools, synagogues, and other institutions, they provided for special councils and courts to administer the laws contained in the Bible, Talmud and other rabbinical code books. Thus, it was Orthodox Judaism which regulated the lives of our people."

Judaism Requires Change. "But the day eventually came," Betty explained, "when many of the Jews won their freedom. Beginning in 1789, the French Revolution gradually brought citizenship to our people in a number of countries, and with their emancipation, Jews began to discover that modern conditions made it impossible for them to practice their former ghetto Judaism. Those who had to work for a living on the Sabbath, for instance, could not attend Saturday worship. Those who no longer resided near the synagogue found it impossible to walk to Sabbath services. Most Jews attended public schools and colleges and had far less time to devote to Jewish study. Hence they were unable to understand the all-Hebrew ritual.

"Furthermore," Betty went on, "conflict arose between the teachings of Orthodox Judaism and the thinking of the modern Jew. Orthodox beliefs in the coming of a personal Messiah and resurrection of the dead, for example, were now regarded as unacceptable.

"The more the Jews became accepted as full citizens of the countries in which they lived, the more they urged that Judaism meet the new conditions of Jewish life. Now that they were subject to the laws of the State, they saw no need for the continuation of many Jewish laws, such as those regulating marriage and divorce, which had governed ghetto life. They sought to make synagogue worship more attractive through the use of the organ, mixed choir, and the language with which they were familiar, and they called for religious ceremonies and customs that were more meaningful to modern Jews.

"Yet," Betty disclosed, "while more and more Jews were becoming dissatisfied with Judaism as it was, Orthodox leaders resisted every demand for change. Increasing numbers of our people began avoiding the synagogue; some even gave up their faith and accepted Christianity. Unless something were soon done to modernize our religion, it seemed as if Judaism would really suffer."

Could Judaism Be Changed? "The first question that had to be settled was whether Judaism permitted change. Reform leaders insisted that it did, and they based their argument upon the needs of the modern Jew and the discoveries of Jewish historians who had proved that our religion had always adjusted to the new conditions of different ages. The Talmud, itself, they declared, represented such an attempt to meet new circumstances.

"The Orthodox, on the other hand, strongly objected to the slightest revision of Jewish practice or belief. They insisted that the Bible, Talmud, and other Jewish sourcebooks had been handed down by God, and, as such, could be changed only by God. Judaism in its present form was established for all times and every attempt at change must be regarded as a violation of God's teachings. Thus, while the early Reformers succeeded in introducing some changes into Jewish worship, the Orthodox continued their opposition with protests to the government and public condemnation of Jews who participated in Reform worship.

"Nevertheless," Betty explained, "the early Reform leaders continued with their program. They organized Reform societies and congregations in some of the larger cities of Germany, England, Hungary, and elsewhere, and in addition to the revision of Orthodox practices, they created new religious ceremonies, like Confirmation. Soon special rabbinical conferences and synods met to consider the question of Jewish observance for modern Jews. A number of important issues were considered—the amount of Hebrew to be used in services, the preservation of the Sabbath in view of modern conditions, revision of Jewish mourning customs, and other problems—and many necessary changes were adopted."

Reform Turns to America. "But there were several reasons why the Reform movement failed to make satisfactory progress in Europe. One was the political reaction which set in following the defeat of Napoleon in 1815. For, no sooner had some of the former kings regained their thrones than they reintroduced many of the anti-Jewish regulations of ghetto days. Jews found further cause for insecurity in the rise of modern anti-Semitism. Under these circumstances, it was natural that the growth of Reform Judaism, which had come into existence to meet the needs of emancipated Jews, should suffer. But the movement's progress was also hindered by powerful Orthodox opposition, the rise of the Conservative movement, and Reform's own failure to create a common religious program or strong, unifying organization.

"It was in the United States that Reform achieved its greatest development," Betty stated. "Here the movement found advantages that it had lacked in Europe. Orthodox opposition was by no means as powerful; organized anti-Semitism was practically unknown; Conservatism was as yet undeveloped and, most important of all, the American Jew enjoyed complete freedom. Reform leaders who now came from Europe already found a Reform congregation in Charleston and Reform societies in some of the larger cities. They quickly turned their energies to the formation of new Reform congregations among the German Jews who comprised most of American Jewry.

"By 1885, American Reform had developed its own program of principles in the Pittsburgh Platform. In it Reform was described as the continuing development of a Judaism which had always changed to meet the needs of each generation of our people. Only by adjusting to modern life could Judaism remain a living religion and enable its followers to carry on their mission of spreading Israel's truths about God and His laws of righteousness, justice, and peace."

The Development of American Reform Judaism. "The Reform movement in the United States continued to grow," Betty went on. "Many more new congregations were founded, and others that were originally Orthodox came to accept Reform. Due to the efforts of Rabbi Isaac Mayer Wise, American Reform created strong national organizations to unite the movement and promote its development. By the beginning of this century the Union of American Hebrew Congregations, the Hebrew Union College and the Central Conference of American Rabbis were well established, and more and more Reform congregations were coming into existence.

"Reform had already made many important contributions to American Jewish life. Its program of religious education, the creation of the first American rabbinical seminary, the building of some of America's most beautiful synagogues, the development of new and meaningful religious practices, the leadership of the Reform rabbinate in major causes of world and American Jewish life, and the religious organizations which it developed through its union of congregations and conference of rabbis were recognized as some of the outstanding Reform achievements.

"Beginning with the 1930's and because of the changed circumstances of Jewish life, many Reform leaders began calling for the creation of a new platform. To them, the Pittsburgh Platform no longer expressed the more recent developments within Reform Judaism. By now, the movement had outgrown its early revolutionary extremes and had been greatly influenced by the attitudes of the more recent immigrants who comprised the vast majority of American Jewry. Then, too, the older Reform ideas were being modified by the growing enthusiasm for the creation of a Jewish Homeland in Palestine, the rise of organized anti-Semitism and the terrible persecution of European Jewry. Most leaders now felt that a new platform was essential to continued Reform progress.

"Therefore, in 1937," Betty asserted, "the Central Conference of American Rabbis adopted 'The

Guiding Principles of Reform Judaism.' Based on the teachings of historical Judaism, the new Reform platform is divided into three major sections—beliefs, ethics, and religious observances. While it contains many of the principles of the Pittsburgh Platform, it likewise includes a number of new ideas. It stresses the duty of Reform Jews to carry on regular religious observance in home and synagogue, the need for ceremonials and symbols in worship, the greater use of Hebrew in services and religious education, and the obligation of every Jew to participate in all worth while Jewish causes, including that of rebuilding Palestine. Today, the new platform serves as the official statement of Reform principles for the more than 500 congregations and the 700,000 Jews affiliated with the movement.

"What's more," Betty concluded, "Reform Judaism is now a world movement with its own international organization, The World Union for Progressive Judaism. As the result of its work, Reform has spread to other countries outside of Europe and North America. Today, there are Reform or 'Liberal' congregations in India, Israel, South Africa, Australia, South America, and other lands.'"

Some Major Reform Accomplishments. Mildred had listened with great interest to the story that Betty told. "What would you say are some of Reform Judaism's most important accomplishments?" she asked Betty.

Betty thought a moment. Then she answered, "I would list, first of all, Reform's belief in a constantly developing Judaism. By emphasizing the historic principle of change in Judaism, Reform has advanced our religion from the period when Jews were compelled to live in ghettos to the present age of American Jewish freedom and citizenship, and, therefore, has made it possible for many modern Jews to practice their religion.

"Secondly," Betty continued, "Reform has brought back to their religion many of our people who had already lost interest in the old forms of Judaism. Had Reform not been created, they might never have joined a synagogue or participated in Jewish life. Today, however, through their discovery of Reform they have once again become active Jews.

"Thirdly," Betty enumerated, "not only has Reform modernized traditional Jewish practices, but it has also supplied a great many new and inspiring features to synagogue worship and Jewish religious life. It has insisted, for instance, upon orderly, dignified services, the regular weekly sermon, and the use of English in prayers. It has created new religious music, introduced the mixed choir and instrumental music in worship, and produced new ceremonies, like Confirmation and Consecration. In addition, it has made many valuable

AMERICAN REFORM DEVELOPMENTS—FROM 1870

Important Happenings in Jewish Life	Major European Reform Events	Reform Developments in America
	1871—Augsburg Synod 1872—Founding of the Liberal Rabbinical Seminary in Berlin	1873—Formation of the Union of American Hebrew Congregations 1875—Founding of the Hebrew Union College
1881—Beginning of pogroms against Russian Jews and mass immigration to the United States		1883—First graduation from the Hebrew Union College 1885—Pittsburgh Rabbinical Conference 1889—Formation of the Central Conference of American Rabbis 1892—Publication of the *Union Prayerbook*
1894—Beginning of the Dreyfus Affair (to 1906) 1897—Formation of the World Zionist Organization	1899—Formation of the Union of Liberal Rabbis in Germany 1903—Founding of the Union Israélite Liberale in Paris 1909—Organization of the Jewish Religious Union in England	1913—Organization of the National Federation of Temple Sisterhoods 1914—Publication of the *Union Hymnal* 1916—Publication of the *Rabbi's Manual* 1922—Founding of the Jewish Institute of Religion 1923—Organization of the National Federation of Temple Brotherhoods
1933—Hitler seizes control of Germany and persecution of Jews begins	1926—Formation of the World Union for Progressive Judaism 1929—Adoption of a common Reform prayer book in Germany	1937—Adoption of "The Guiding Principles of Reform Judaism" 1939—Organization of the National Federation of Temple Youth
1948—Founding of the State of Israel	1955—Creation of Liberal Rabbinical Seminary in Paris	1950—Merger of the Hebrew Union College and Jewish Institute of Religion 1951—Dedication of the Union's House of Living Judaism

contributions to American Jewish religious life, such as the creation of a modern rabbinate, the development of a complete program and literature for religious education, and the production of new architectural forms for the synagogue.

"Fourthly," she stated, "not only has our movement reemphasized traditional Jewish beliefs such as Israel's Mission to all mankind and the importance of social justice, but it has also introduced new principles into Judaism. Reform, for example, champions equal religious rights for Jewish women and maintains that our religion is in agreement with scientific discovery.

"And lastly," she concluded, "there's Reform's contribution to all phases of Jewish religious life in America. More and more non-Reform congregations, for instance, have adopted Confirmation, the late Friday evening service, and other Reform practices; and a large number use Reform religious school textbooks, courses of study, programs of teacher training and adult education materials. Both the Orthodox and Conservative movements, too, have patterned their national organization on the Reform model. They have their unions of congregations, rabbinical seminaries and conferences, associations of synagogue women and youth. The Reform movement, as you can see, has had enormous influence upon the development of Judaism in America."

"And That's the Story of Reform Judaism. . . ." By now it had grown quite late. For several moments Mildred said nothing. Then she turned to her friend and said thoughtfully, "So that's the story. . . ."

"Yes," Betty answered as she rose to leave, "that's the story of Reform Judaism. . . ."

QUESTIONS FOR DISCUSSION

1. In what ways has Jewish life changed since ghetto times?
2. Why did the early Reformers consider it essential to modify Orthodox medieval Judaism?
3. What answers has Reform to those who regard Judaism as unchangeable?
4. Why did Reform in the United States make greater progress than the movement in Europe?
5. How did Reform Judaism originate in your community?
6. What are some of the important Reform contributions to American Jewish life today?

SUGGESTED ACTIVITIES

1. Prepare a booklet for non-Reform young people on the subject: "How Reform Judaism Came to Be."
2. Create a series of illustrated posters presenting outstanding Reform contributions to American Jewish life.
3. Prepare a talk for the school assembly or religious service on the subject: "What Reform Judaism Means to Me."

ADDITIONAL READINGS FOR PUPILS

CONOVITZ, MICHAEL, *Dorothy and David Explore Jewish Life*, pp. 166-173.

FEUER, LEON I. and AZRIEL EISENBERG, *Jewish Literature Since the Bible, II*, pp. 206-210.

GOLUB, JACOB S. and ALAN S. GREEN, *A Short History of the Jews, III*, p. 48.

References for the Teacher

FREEHOF, SOLOMON B., *Reform Jewish Practice*, "Introduction."

Jewish Encyclopedia, "Reform Judaism from the Point of View of the Reform Jew," Vol. 10, pp. 347-352.

SCHWARTZMAN, SYLVAN D., *Reform Judaism in the Making*, Chap. 1, "Reform and the Jewish Future"; Chap. 17, "This Is Reform Judaism."

Universal Jewish Encyclopedia, "Judaism in America (Reform Judaism)," Vol. 6, pp. 240-243; "Reform Movement," Vol. 9, pp. 101-103.

BIBLIOGRAPHY

ABRAHAMS, ISRAEL, *Jewish Life in the Middle Ages,* Edward Goldston, Ltd., London, 1932.

American Jewish Archives, Vols. I-IV, Hebrew Union College, Cincinnati, 1948–1952.

American Jewish Yearbook, 52 Vols., Jewish Publication Society, Philadelphia.

American Judaism, 2 Vols., Union of American Hebrew Congregations, New York, 1952–1953.

Annual Reports, 75 years, Union of American Hebrew Congregations, New York.

BEIN, ALEX, *Theodor Herzl,* Jewish Publication Society, Philadelphia, 1942.

COHEN, ISRAEL, *The Zionist Movement,* Marstin Press, New York, 1946.

COHON, BERYL D., *Judaism in Theory and Practice,* Bloch Publishing Co., New York, 1948.

COHON, SAMUEL S., "The History of the Hebrew Union College," Publications of the American Jewish Historical Society, XL, Part 1, September, 1950.

——, *What We Jews Believe,* Union of American Hebrew Congregations, New York, 1931.

Conference Volumes, World Union for Progressive Judaism, 6 issues, London.

EGELSON, LOUIS I., Reform Judaism—A Movement of the People, Union of American Hebrew Congregations, New York, 1949.

ELBOGEN, ISMAR, *A Century of Jewish Life,* Jewish Publication Society, Philadelphia, 1944.

FELSENTHAL, EMMA, *Bernhard Felsenthal—Teacher in Israel,* Oxford University Press, New York, 1924.

FREEHOF, SOLOMON B., *Reform Jewish Practice,* Hebrew Union College Press, Cincinnati, 1944.

——, What Is Reform Judaism? Union of American Hebrew Congregations, New York.

FREIMANN, ARON and FELIX KRACAUER, *History of the Jews of Frankfort,* Jewish Publication Society, Philadelphia, 1929.

GAMORAN, EMANUEL, *Changing Conceptions in Jewish Education,* Macmillan, New York, 1924.

GAMORAN, EMANUEL, IRVING M. LEVEY and EMIL W. LEIPZIGER, What He Created, Union of American Hebrew Congregations, New York, 1946.

GOLDEN, HARRY L. and MARTIN RYWELL, *Jews in American History,* Henry Lewis Martin Company, Charlotte, 1950.

GRAETZ, HEINRICH, *History of the Jews,* 6 Vols., Jewish Publication Society, Philadelphia, 1891–1898.

GUTHEIM, JAMES K., Cause, Development and Scope of Reform (Sermon), Bloch Publishing Co., New York, 1886.

HACKER, LOUIS M. and BENJAMIN B. HENDRICK, *The United States Since 1865,* Crofts, New York, 1935.

Hebrew Union College–Jewish Institute of Religion Catalogue, Cincinnati and New York, 1952.

HELLER, BERNARD, *The Odyssey of a Faith,* Harper and Brothers, New York, 1942.

HIRSCH, SAMSON RAPHAEL, *The Nineteen Letters of Ben Uziel,* translated by Bernard Drachman, Funk and Wagnalls, New York, 1899.

HYAMSON, ALBERT M. and A. M. SILBERMANN, *Jewish Encyclopaedia,* Shapiro, Vallentine and Company, London, 1938.

Jewish Encyclopedia, 12 Vols., Funk and Wagnalls, New York, 1901.

JOSEPH, MORRIS, *Judaism as Creed and Life,* Macmillan, New York, 1919.

KOBER, ADOLF, *History of Jews in Cologne,* Jewish Publication Society, Philadelphia, 1940.

KOHLER, KAUFMANN, *Hebrew Union College and Other Addresses,* Ark Publishing Co., Cincinnati, 1916.

—— *Jewish Theology,* Macmillan, New York, 1928.

——, *Studies, Addresses and Personal Papers,* Bloch Publishing Co., New York, 1931.

KRAUSKOPF, JOSEPH, Lectures, 1888–1889, Philadelphia.

LAZARUS, O., *Liberal Judaism and Its Standpoint,* Macmillan, London, 1937.

LEVINGER, LEE J., *A History of the Jews in the United States,* Union of American Hebrew Congregations, New York, 1949.

LEVY, BERYL HAROLD, *Reform Judaism in America,* Bloch Publishing Co., New York, 1933.

Liberal Judaism, 19 Vols., Union of American Hebrew Congregations, New York, 1943–1951.

LOWENTHAL, MARVIN, *The Jews of Germany,* Jewish Publication Society, Philadelphia, 1936.

MARCUS, JACOB R., *The Jew in the Medieval World,* Sinai Press, Cincinnati, 1938.

——, *The Rise and Destiny of the German Jew,* Union of American Hebrew Congregations, New York, 1934.

MARGOLIS, MAX L. and ALEXANDER MARX, *A History of the Jewish People,* Jewish Publication Society, Philadelphia, 1927.

MARKENS, ISAAC, *The Hebrews in America,* Bloch Publishing Co., New York, 1888.

MASSERMAN, PAUL and MAX BAKER, *The Jews Come to America,* Bloch Publishing Co., New York, 1932.

MAY, MAX B., *Isaac Mayer Wise,* Putnam, New York, 1916.

Menorah, 42 Vols., Menorah Publishing Company, New York, 1886–1907.

MORGENSTERN, JULIAN, *As a Mighty Stream,* Jewish Publication Society, Philadelphia, 1949.

Occident, The, Philadelphia, 1843–1869.

PHILIPSON, DAVID, *Centenary Papers and Others,* Ark Publishing Co., Cincinnati, 1919.

——, *Max Lilienthal,* Bloch Publishing Co., New York, 1915.

——, *The Reform Movement in Judaism,* Macmillan, New York, 1931.

Rabbi's Manual, Central Conference of American Rabbis, Cincinnati, 1928.

Reform Judaism, Essays by Alumni of the Hebrew Union College, Hebrew Union College Press, Cincinnati, 1949.

REZNIKOFF, CHARLES and URIAH Z. ENGELMAN, *The Jews of Charleston,* Jewish Publication Society, Philadelphia, 1950.

ROTH, CECIL, *A Bird's-Eye View of Jewish History,* Union of American Hebrew Congregations, New York, 1935.

——, *History of Jews in Venice,* Jewish Publication Society, Philadelphia, 1930.

SACHAR, ABRAM LEON, *A History of the Jews,* Knopf, New York, 1948.

SCHAPIRO, J. SALWYN, *Modern and Contemporary European History,* Houghton Mifflin Co., Cambridge, 1931.

SCHRIEBER, EMANUEL, *Reformed Judaism and Its Pioneers,* Spokane Printing Co., Spokane, 1892.

SCHWARTZMAN, SYLVAN D., *Reform Judaism in the Making,* Union of American Hebrew Congregations, New York, 1951.

STEINBERG, MILTON, *The Making of the Modern Jew,* Behrman's Jewish Book House, New York, 1943.

Universal Jewish Encyclopedia, ed. Isaac Landman, The Universal Jewish Encyclopedia, New York, 1939.

WIERNIK, PETER, *History of the Jews in America,* The Jewish History Publishing Co., New York, 1931.

WISE, ISAAC M., *Reminiscences,* Leo Wise and Co., Cincinnati, 1901.

Yearbook, Central Conference of American Rabbis, 61 Vols.

INDEX

UNION GRADED SERIES

EDITED BY

EMANUEL GAMORAN, PH.D., *Director of Education*
Union of American Hebrew Congregations